gardens in

NORMANDY

MARIE-FRANÇOISE VALÉRY

PHOTOGRAPHY BY VINCENT MOTTE

AND CHRISTIAN SARRAMON

Flammarion
Paris - New York

Translated by Tamara Blondel
Copyediting by Christa Weil
Proof reading by Camille Cloutier

Editorial direction: Ghislaine Bavoillot
Designed by Marc Walter
Origination by Colourscan, France
Typesetting by Octavo Editions, Paris
Printed in Italy by Canale, Turin

Flammarion
26, rue Racine
75006 Paris

ISBN: 2-08013-579-1
Numéro d'édition: 0933
Dépôt légal: March 1995

CONTENTS

— 7 —

A BLUE, WHITE, AND GREEN LAND

— 21 —

FLOWER GARDENS

— 75 —

AROUND A CHÂTEAU

— 103 —

ENGLISH STYLE

— 127 —

WATER GARDENS

— 149 —

GOURMET GARDENS

— 173 —

COLLECTORS' GARDENS

— 201 —

VISITOR'S GUIDE

A Blue,
White, and
Green Land

Normandy has continuously been a fertile source of artistic inspiration. Guy de Maupassant, who was born there in the château of Miromesnil, chose it as the setting for his best novels, tales, and short stories. Gustave Flaubert did likewise for his great novel, *Madame Bovary*, and the region may well have inspired Claude Debussy's composition *Jardins sous la pluie*. In Normandy, Jean de La Varende created a chess game made out of topiary and Jacques Prévert planted a garden by the sea.

Jacques-Emile Blanche, a portrait painter of British gentry and of the Proustian circle in Paris, loved this province as much as he did England. Elisabeth de Gramont, in her *Souvenirs du Monde*, relates: "in front of his house in Dieppe, [Blanche] replaced Oscar Wilde's sunflowers with fields of white poppies which stood out against the blue of the sea, like a beautiful painting." She evokes the old Norman farm where the artist lived and also his Elizabethan garden which, in the summer, was filled with bright flowers: balsam (*Impatiens balsamina*), hollyhock (alcea), sweet william (*Dianthus barbatus*), campanula (commonly known as bellflowers), and larkspur (consolida) mingling with cultivated roses.

"This county is paradise," wrote the painter Frédéric Bazille. Claude Monet adopted it and James McNeill Whistler, the American artist and friend of Gustave Courbet, frequented the Saint-Siméon farm in Honfleur where Impressionists were in the habit of gathering and where he also painted many beautiful landscapes. Camille Pissarro's *Pommiers et Peupliers au soleil couchant* portrays an idyllic image of Normandy. Here he renders the Auge region, with its pasturelands and woods and shadows. A Normandy suffused with the pleasant smell of apples, always green and fresh. As at Criqueboeuf, where the actor Yul Brynner created an English-style garden structured by hedges; rooms of greenery enclose a golden garden, a water garden, a kitchen garden, and a fragrant flower garden.

The scenery, however, is not always quite so perfect. Civilization advances and devours the countryside. Chaos sets in. At the Château d'Orcher, near Le Havre, two worlds confront each other: the greenery of the castle grounds and the iron of the industries below. Luckily there is a strong movement to preserve the charm of Normandy, and to maintain the gardens as they were in the past in a beautiful setting.

Today, the painter Patrick Waravka draws inspiration from the magical play of water and the movement of foliage which takes place in his garden in Varengeville-sur-Mer, which he then reproduces in his pictures. Artists are attracted by the Norman light, which is abetted by the sea. It bathes the flowers and the colors in a white light. "When I leave Trouville I feel as though the light diminishes," wrote Marguerite Duras. "Not only the bright sunshine but also the diffuse white light from overcast or stormy skies. When far from here at the end of the summer, I miss the skies which come from under the Atlantic . . ."

The Impressionists captured all the facets of the reflections created by the mist, that luminous mist which drains the color from nature. They captured the magic of the rain. Maupassant, who met Monet in Etretat in 1885, relates: "he seized a shower beating down on the sea and threw it onto the canvas. And it was indeed the rain that he painted, nothing but the rain masking waves, rocks and sky which were almost indistinguishable in the deluge."

Eugène Boudin, the celebrated painter of Honfleur, was consecrated "king of the skies" by his contemporaries. He knew how to portray this moving, ever-changing sky, this diaphanous, pale, fleecy, or leaden vault, which enhances the green tones and the colors of the flowers and creates a bridge between the two. The pastel gardens harmonize with this sky and the bright colors cause it to vibrate. Blue, white, and gray, the sky transforms before the wind. It brings a

With their delicate, flat flowers the Hydrangea macrophylla 'Blue Wave' are very elegant (page 1). Hydrangea macrophylla, here with domed heads, illuminate the half-timbering of this beautiful manor house situated in Limésy in the Caux region (pages 2–3). Roses, so highly prized by the impressionist painters who stayed in Normandy, stand up well to this damp climate; this book enables one to discover numerous rose gardens (page 4). Apple trees with their pink petals buffeted by the wind and rain of a spring day— just as evoked by Marcel Proust—flower in a valley in the Auge region, not far from Lisieux (previous pages).

The Criqueboeuf manor garden in the Auge region was created by Yul Brynner. Behind the manor house, the vegetation grows freely and a creeper crawls up and cascades down the walls (facing page). In front of the manor house, typically Norman apple trees adorn a beautiful green carpet. The half-timbering is set off by yew hedges which frame the façade on each side (above). In the wild garden, the first flowers to bloom in the spring are the primulas. Here, a spectacular clump of auricula (Primula auricula, below).

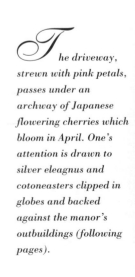

The driveway, strewn with pink petals, passes under an archway of Japanese flowering cherries which bloom in April. One's attention is drawn to silver eleagnus and cotoneasters clipped in globes and backed against the manor's outbuildings (following pages).

beneficial mist. Veils of rain refresh the summers and make the winters milder. Gardens revive under the showers. The foliage and the flowers are invigorated—unless the sea gets angry. For the sea has its mildness and its balminess, but also has its storms.

Normandy is a blue, white, and green garden. Blue like the sea, like the sky in fine weather, or the flax fields in the Caux region. The flax comes into bloom at the beginning of the summer, offering fragile, supple, and ephemeral corollas of a heavenly blue. White like chalk, or the cliffs of the Côte Fleurie, like apple blossoms, milk, seafoam, or fresh cream. Green like its forests, its meadows, and its woodlands. Like its pastures which are the grazing grounds for the dappled Percherons, heavy but well-balanced, the cobs and trotters, and the elegant, haughty thoroughbred, prince of the racecourses.

In the Heart of the Norman Countryside

This vast province covers no less than five departments: the Seine-Maritime and the Eure in Upper Normandy; and the Manche, the Calvados, and the Orne in Lower Normandy. It is bordered to the north by the Channel coast and traversed by the river Seine. The river is a world unto itself. It traces gentle meanders, then angular loops before reaching the estuary and flowing into the sea. The coastline itself is white, like chalk or sand. Each region has its

coast: for instance the Côte Opale or Albâtre along the palisaded boundary of the Caux region, the Côte Fleurie near Honfleur, and the Côte Nacre beyond the river Orne. It is rocky in the Cotentin region and sandy towards Mont-Saint-Michel.

The landscapes in Normandy offer infinite nuances, and the various soil categories explain the multiplicity of the gardens. In his work *Nez-de-Cuir*, Jean de La Varende bears witness to this diversity. "Like the rising tide, smooth and oblique, the vast expanse of the Ouche plateau mounts gradually towards the south until suddenly it breaks like a wave, plunging into the Perche region in a cascade of hills and a swirl of gorges and rifts filled with rushing water, pools, and babbling streams."

The Bray region in Upper Normandy is a land of orchards and pastures. Riddled with woods and beech groves, the landscape literally brightens in the spring with budding hawthorn hedges and blossoming apple and pear trees. This is the region described by Flaubert in *Madame Bovary*: "the water that flows along the edge of the grass, separates the color of the meadows from that of the furrows by a white stripe making the countryside look like a large unfolded coat with a velvet cape edged in silver braid." On the chalky plateaus of the Norman Vexin and Caux regions, the rivers trace furrows of greenery. This is the country of open fields and dilapidated farmhouses, the vast farmsteads often protected by beech ramparts. It also possesses a spectacular coastline with impressive white cliffs stretching from Etretat to Dieppe. The Ouche region, on the other

When writing Madame Bovary, Flaubert recollected the yellows, blues, and violets reflected in the rivers, as well as the good country smells so typical of the landscape of the Bray and the Caux regions (here the banks of the Varenne).

This flax field situated between Bailleul and Fécamp is characteristic of the Caux region. Flax is cultivated for decorative purposes, for its oil, and for the textile industry. The beautiful blue flowers are short-lived, graceful, supple, fragile, and fresh (facing page).

hand, harbors deep, damp forests; it is a greener, more secretive region, dotted with centuries-old farms and isolated manor houses.

In Lower Normandy, the Cotentin unfolds its moors, marshes, and meadows. Barbey d'Aureville, in his work *L'Ensorcelée*, evokes the Lessay moors and expresses his astonishment at their "lack of cultivation: like arid oases in these fertile lands, just as there are green oases in the arid desert sands. They make sudden melancholy interruptions in this fresh, gay, fertile scenery. They give it a worried, severe aspect and shadow it with a darker tone . . ." Nevertheless, in this county bordered by the sea, the mild, damp climate makes it possible for palm trees to be grown.

As to the valleys of the river Orne, they abound with forests of beech, oak, and Scots pine. In the Vire district, the Norman farmland looks like a puzzle in green. In this very distinctive landscape, where hedges have progressively divided up the pastures, trees and wild shrubs mingle and cover the hills. One can get lost in the sunken lanes which thread their way between high walls of greenery. This is traditional Normandy, a checkerboard landscape, punctuated with farms, barns, manor houses, and villages.

Approaching the region known as the Suisse Nor-mande, the wooded landscape is scored by wild gorges and high cliffs. Then one reaches the Auge district, which is the heart of this beautiful province. With its greenswards and apple trees, it is a damp, fresh, pastoral universe. Here all the contours are rounded: the tops of the apple trees, the apples themselves, the balls of mistletoe, the hills . . . only the church steeples stand out. They punctuate the landscape with their elongated tapering silhouettes which appear and disappear. Marcel Proust's evocation of this typically Norman ballet is superb: "Alone, standing out above the uniform level of the plain and as though lost in the open country, the two steeples of Saint-Etienne rose towards the sky. Soon we saw three of them, the steeple of Saint-Pierre had joined them. . . . The minutes passed . . . and yet the three steeples were still in front of us, alone, like immobile birds on the plain, clearly visible in the sun. Then . . . the towers of the Trinité appeared, or rather only one tower, so exactly did it mask the one behind it. Then it moved, the other one advanced and both appeared in line."

The various types of soil determine the particular gardens which flower at the foot of a steeple or nestle in the countryside. Typical of the province are chalky soils, clayey or acidic patches, and humidity.

In the coastal regions, gardens are either found sheltering in the valleys, or burgeoning under the influence of the mild Gulf Stream, which fosters luxuriant subtropical vegetation.

Which plants are to be found in Normandy? First of all the noble and majestic beeches. They are often perched on embankments, curiously enough called "ditches" in this region (since a ditch needs to be dug in order to build an embankment). Trees were planted on the embankments in order to retain the soil and their protruding tentacular roots are quite visible. Beeches are favored for this practice, notably in the Caux region.

Next come the apple trees—the symbols of this province. "As soon as I reached the road I was met by a dazzling sight," relates Marcel Proust. "There, where with my grandmother in August, I had seen merely the leaves and the position of the apple trees, now as far as the eye could see, they were in full bloom. An incredible luxury with their feet in the mud, but dressed for a ball and taking no precautions to protect the most magnificent pink satin that has ever been seen glistening in the sun . . ." The apple trees are in blossom at the end of April or the beginning of May. The buds are pink, the flowers, white. The first crop of fruit is gathered in the autumn, the last one at the beginning of December. Sparkling, slightly foamy cider is produced, or the powerful Calvados, which is drunk in the middle of a festive meal—the famous *trou Normand*. Pommeau is another Norman specialty consisting of a mixture of apple juice and Calvados, and is drunk as an aperitif.

Then there are the famous trees, those that everyone here knows. For instance in the Patry moor in the Orne department, there is a yew tree which measures more than ten meters in circumference. Also in the Orne, the oak tree at the Ferme du Tertre in Tellières-le-Plessis, which is reputed to be more than four hundred years old. The Offranville yew tree, near Dieppe, is said to date from the end of the ninth century, and the "Liberty" plane tree in Bayeux was set into the ground in 1797.

Thistles, pink-flowering *Geranium robertianum*, enormous prickly brambles, hawthorns and elders overrun with bearded silver clematis, thrive in this green countryside. Salix, gorse, rushes, and meadow-sweet grow in the damp ditches. These wild plants are the cousins of those to be found in the gardens. They like the same soil and the same sky. Garden lovers can therefore cultivate an infinite range of perennial plants, from the commonest to the rarest and most sought after. They flower over a long period, from spring to autumn and even in winter: from the helleborus or Christmas rose, which blossoms in January or February; to the aster, which flowers until the first frosts; not to mention the Japanese primulas, irises, peonies, perennial geraniums, phlox, hemerocallis (commonly called daylilies), and campanulas. All prosper under the Norman skies. So too do more exotic varieties like the meconopsis (known as the blue poppy), a heavenly blue flower that was discovered in the Himalayas. They are also grown in Scotland and we are lucky to be able to enjoy them in France due to the exceptionally mild, fresh, damp, and shady climate of Normandy.

Large quantities of bulbs are to be found in these gardens: crocuses, squills, fritillaries, alliums, lilies, and colchicum, commonly known as meadow saffron. There is also a wide range of trees and shrubs, among which figure magnolias and dogwood (cornus) and especially rhododendrons and hydrangeas, whose often fragile, delicate floral elegance, fleeting yet regular and prolific, is the crowning glory of Norman gardens. Normandy lends itself to opulence and to the profusion of flowers and foliage.

The Tradition of a Floral Paradise

What image of paradise can one conjure up in Normandy? In the past, local gardens did not hew to any well-defined tradition. There were monastery gardens, but also abbey, priory, farm, cottage, manor house, and castle gardens. Notwithstanding their varying configurations and purposes, they all sprang from common ground. With its mild climate, abundant rainfall, and rich soil, Normandy is ideal garden country. Today the province is home to an even broader panoply of historical, traditional, and showcase gardens.

One of the first masterpieces of the gardening art to emerge appears to have been Gaillon,

near Vernon, in the Eure department. Conceived at the beginning of the sixteenth century around the magnificent château of the bishops of Rouen, it was one of the first Renaissance gardens to be created in France. Although inspired by medieval themes, it was ornate, sophisticated, and aromatic. Hardly anything now remains except the plans drawn up by Androuet du Cerceau. However, its renown was such that it has served as reference for many gardens and it is now hoped that it will be possible to restore it.

Charleval, situated in the same department, is reputed to be one of the first great classic gardens. Started at the end of the sixteenth century, it was symmetrically designed around a central axis and integrated with the castle's architecture. Here again, all that remains are Androuet du Cerceau's plans.

From this rich past, a few marvels remain. In the Norman Vexin, the property known as Heudicourt testifies to the evolution of the horticultural art in the seventeenth century, and offers a vision of the gardens of the "Grand Siècle." Approached by magnificent *allées* bordered by planes and lindens, the gardens are of classical inspiration. Paths fan out in a star shape from a central axis which commands flowerbeds, copses, a green foliage theater, a riding ring, and perspectives opening onto the countryside thanks to strategically placed hahas (sunken fences that preserve views while preventing the passage of livestock). Influenced by the new fashion of the period, gardens at the back of the castle were laid out in the English style, with clumps of trees disseminated freely throughout the park. There was even a project for an Anglo-Chinese garden at Heudicourt, with rocks, summerhouses, and sophisticated pavilions, but this plan never materialized.

The English style imposed itself in many Norman castle grounds, one example being Beaurepaire in the Cotentin, created by the comte de Moncel in 1820. Waterfalls continue to cascade, and so do the rhododendrons. Clusters of oaks, beeches, and cypresses follow the winding paths and the meandering river. They grow side by side with exotic species, notably palm trees.

Everything is possible in Normandy: a Scottish landscape, a subtropical décor, a French-style park, or a Mediterranean-style garden with gray foliage. The latter in the Calvados,

where the landscape gardener Louis Benech designed a garden around a swimming pool. There one can admire the clipped domes of silver eleagnus, *Senecio grayi*, woolly santolina and *Choisya ternata* (known as Mexican orange blossom). Masses of white flowers emerge everywhere: roses, hydrangeas, dahlias, and Japanese anemones on a silvery white carpet of snow-in-summer (*Cerastium tomentosum*). This garden was too recent to be photographed, but holds promise of some beautiful surprises.

The world of Norman gardens is growing and becoming richer. Historic gardens are being restored and all sorts of contemporary gardens are seeing the light of day. Among those who are fascinated by this art in Normandy are three emblematic figures to whom tribute must be paid: Princesse Greta Sturdza, Mary Mallet, and her son Robert Mallet.

Princesse Sturdza worships her garden, Vasterival, near Varengeville-sur-Mer. She has designed it to be beautiful in all seasons, even in winter. A highly skilled botanist, she has transmitted her love of plants and beautiful gardens to everyone. Needless to say, her influence is felt far beyond the borders of Normandy. As to Mary Mallet, she was one of the first, in 1970, to open the grounds of her property, Le Bois des Moutiers, in Varengeville, to the public. Conceived at the end of the last century by her father-in-law, Guillaume Mallet, a collector and enlightened art lover, this garden is in the English style and regularly serves as a reference. Robert Mallet, Guillaume's grandson, has made many contributions to the garden world and was notably at the origin of the creation of the Association des Parcs Botaniques de France, the Conservatoire des Collections végétales spécialisées, and of Les Journées de Courson. Thanks to him, quantities of rare plants have been introduced in France.

Normandy excels in the world of gardens. It attracts true afficionados who live their passion to the full. Because of them we can enter into many a paradise: flower gardens, water gardens, gourmet gardens, collector's gardens. This region is full of magic and promise. As the duc de Broglie pointed out in his introduction to *Le Pays d'Ouche* by Jean de La Varende, "the Normans, perhaps more than others, are very aware of the supernatural qualities inherent in nature."

FLOWER GARDENS

Countless varieties of flowers thrive under the skies of Normandy. Whether in bunches, spires, or umbels; single or double; wild or cultivated; translucent, fleshy, or glossy; the juxtaposition creates magnificent effects—pointillist or impressionistic tableaux which are the charm of the gardens of Normandy. The gardeners like the range of soft and vivid colors, and they know how to orchestrate mono- or polychromatic arrays against a beautiful deep green backdrop.

The trees, shrubs, lawns, hedges, and foliage plants together offer the entire range of greens, the tones and half tones expressed with exceptional subtlety. The subdued light and the rain are favorable to annuals, bulbs, perennials, and flowering shrubs. The flowerbeds bedeck themselves with multitudes of petals. Such profusion! When one adds the fragrances, a thematic puzzle to decipher, the harmony between a garden and an old half-timbered manor house trellised with flowering creeper, both vision and intellect are gratified.

Because of the architectural structure of these gardens, they show all flowers off to advantage. The geometrical symmetry of the design contrasts with the comparatively random nonchalance of the plantings. The flowerbeds are nearly always planted against a wall or a dark hedge which brings out the colors.

The flowers are chosen with a precise objective: to illustrate a theme, to harmonize with a site, to be beautiful at one particular time, or to relate to each other almost all the year round. They are chosen for their color, fragrance, height, texture, and foliage; according to the date and duration of their flowering; or again for their architectural value or their simplicity. Above all, of course, they are chosen for their concordance with each other.

These flower gardens are well-suited to the Norman landscape—which Maupassant describes as a floral countryside and which does not seem to have changed since his time. "Here and there the flowering colza formed a vast, billowing yellow tablecloth. Little heads of azure cornflowers peeped out from the tall rye . . . and the white horse trotted along, drawing its cart across the plains painted with the flowers of the earth."

Floral beauty is to be found at Vandrimare, where plant scenes succeed each other in space and time, and also at Giverny, where Monet created a *jardin de curé* in much the same way as he would have composed a painting. "A colorist garden" as Proust described it, where the artist combined all sorts of flowers and colors chosen with care and with particular attention to harmony. Beauty is also to be found at Thury-Harcourt, a garden park created with talent and simplicity, like a garland of flowers on a green carpet.

Some gardens are situated on the coast and therefore need to be protected from the wind by walls or dense hedges. Isabel Canovas, a designer of luxury accessories, protects her roses in this fashion by planting them between clipped yew and box. Sometimes the hedges serve to prevent the fragrances from escaping. This is a fine example of a "showcase" garden. Another is the Prieuré Saint-Michel in the Auge region, where one passes from one compartment to another, from one color to another, and from one fragrance to another.

The flower gardens are designed so as to be in harmony with the style of the houses. In the town of Bailleul, for example, in the Caux region, the Maison Normande is surrounded by flowers and foliage. At Basses Terres in the Dives marsh region, the landscaper Louis Benech (who is restoring the Jardin des Tuileries in Paris), created a mixed border in the best Anglo-Saxon style. The walls of the house are in peach tones, the drawing room is blue and melon-colored, and the mixed border is blue and salmon with a few touches of white. The plants, chosen from among the most gracious varieties, are combined with great nuance. The tones and textures are soft. This nascent site is full of charm and amplitude.

Sometimes flowers are cultivated in order to be put in vases and so a "bouquet" garden is planted. In the Auge region, the Swiss landscape gardener Franz Baechler created a garden enclosed by trellises. In a regular design composed of squares he combined all kinds of varieties that look attractive in a vase: roses, dahlias, asters, multicolored zinnias, phlox, campanulas (commonly known as bellflowers), and larkspur. The paths are grassy. Clematis and honeysuckle climb all over the chestnut trellises. The overall effect is simple, rural, and absolutely charming.

The Auge region is renowned for its half-timbered manor houses, often surrounded by apple trees in the middle of an orchard. This one is situated at the end of a long grassy path, cut in the English style, bordered by ornamental apple trees (above). Three enclosed kitchen gardens are found on the grounds. One enters by small wicket gates below the clipped vegetation archways (center).

In Normandy, flower gardens are full of audacity. Plants which otherwise suffer in cold, such as *Clematis armandii* or ceratostigma, grow unprotected. The mildness of the climate permits these fantasies. This frequent combination of hardy and rare, frost-tender plants is reminiscent of the gardens across the Channel in England, and makes Norman plantings very precious and distinct from other gardens in France.

A Manor House Garden: the Harmony of Flowers and Half-Timbering

At a well-hidden manor house, charming floral scenes planted in boxwood settings at the foot of half-timbered walls were created under the hand and eye of a gardener who masters the subject perfectly. She chose easy plants producing regular abundant flowerings, for she is well aware of the constraints of nature and horticulture. So she created a garden requiring minimum upkeep, after having carefully studied the house and landscape, the axis of the windows, and the proportions of the façade.

The property is situated in Upper Normandy. Dating from the seventeenth century, it is a family manor covered with slate, traditional tile, and thatch roofing. In front of the building, a green geometric architecture consisting of cone-shaped box, which is clipped into green globes in the angles, encloses perennials and shrubs which are densely planted to prevent weeds from proliferating. Pink-flowered perennial geraniums (*G. endressii*), lavender, sages, ferns, mint, and chives produce pastel-colored flowers which harmonize with the wisteria, white *Clematis montana*, and very pale yellow 'Albéric Barbier' rose, which are trained along the half-timbered façade.

Behind the manor is a long avenue planted with ornamental 'Everest' apple trees. Bearing pale pink blossoms in spring and small translucid fruits late in the season, they lead to a vast orchard with rows of traditional apple trees.

Nearby a doll's house, box squirrels, peacocks, bears, and chicks watch over orange, yellow, and red nasturtiums combined with yellow and pale orange "potimarrons," a diminutive member of the pumpkin family.

Around an old well, masses of pink, blue, and mauve-veined white perennial geraniums (like *G. endressii*, *G. macrorrhizum*,

A parterre of flowers surrounded by boxwood affords space for sage, perennial Geranium endressii, santolina, ferns, mint, and chives—and serves as display case for the manor house. The half-timbered façade is covered by an 'Albéric Barbier' climbing rose, a white clematis, and a mauve wisteria (facing page).

G. 'Johnson's Blues', *G. clarkei* 'Kashmir White'), brush up against Old Garden remontant 'Jacques Cartier' roses with their pink, double flowers in quartered rosettes.

Rhododendrons and various perennials stretch as far as the entrance to the kitchen gardens, which contain flowers, fruit, and vegetables.

This garden is the result of a long progression in the world of gardening and the fine arts. It was designed by a master in the art of creating beauty from basic essentials.

A Contemporary Landscape Architect, Louis Benech, Designs the Garden of a Stud Farm

Not far away, behind a white railing enclosing pastureland for grazing horses, stretches the Domaine de La Rivière.

The site is idyllic and enchanting. It smells of apples and freshly cut hay. The flower garden, planted in the midst of an apple grove, is part of a complex including a manor house, cider press, compost barn, dovecote, and stables. These buildings are all half-timbered, and their traditional tiled roofs have acquired a rich patina. They date from the seventeenth century. The English landscape gardener Russell Page, who was designing gardens in Normandy at the time, stayed at the domain for a while as he was a friend of the family, but he didn't make many changes in the gar-

den . . . he merely planted a few trees here and there. The property took on a new life when Louis Benech worked there. He created a woodland garden in a formal design representing a four-leafed clover. He enhanced the dovecote with perennials and flowering creepers in harmony with the white peacock doves that nest there. He enlarged the two beds facing the manor which border a croquet lawn, so as to be able to plant a much wider range of annuals and perennials and to prolong their beauty over the four seasons.

The oak door of the dovecote is flanked by two box globes which combine with ferns and hostas, commonly known as plantain lily. Foxgloves, lupins, willow herbs, foxtail lilies (*Eremurus himalaicus*), Madonna lilies (*Lilium candidum*), royal lilies (*L. regale*), and centaurea (known as knapweed), tone in with the plumage of the peacock doves. Creepers embellish the half-timbering and the wide green leaves of a crimson glory vine (*Vitis coignetiae*) and the variegated cream and pink leaves of *Actinidia kolomikta* keep company with a wisteria.

Two English-style mixed borders are set off by a typical Norman lawn, damp and impeccably green. The borders are prolific and exuberant, simple and light. In winter they are planted with masses of pansies, primulas, and daisies. In spring the beds take on gray and blue tones with touches of white and soft yellow. Forget-me-nots, pansies, and knapweed represent the blue and mauve color range. Snow-in-summer (*Cerastium tomentosum*) forms silver cushions interspersed with tulips. All these flowers are set off by the

In this jardin de curé in front of the bread oven at the Manoir de La Plesse, the plants are lined up in kitchen-garden fashion. They are all traditional and easy to grow. They are disposed in rectangles and each bed contains a single plant variety for the spring, the summer, and the autumn (facing page).

foliage of recently planted perennials which hold out much promise for the future.

In the summer all kinds of herbaceous plants, combined with some of the most elegant annuals, flower without interruption. Lupins, phlox, Japanese anemones, loosestrife (*Lysimachia clethroides*), physostegia (commonly known as obedient plant), gaura, and rudbeckia (or coneflowers) are mixed with cosmos, sages (such as *Salvia farinacea* or *S. horminum*), or even with roses and dahlias to ensure constant colorful flowerings.

This garden is both simple and subtle, soft and rural, green and above all harmonious. It is one of those places where people feel invulnerable because it is like being in paradise. This garden is enriching because it offers a beautiful image which delights the soul.

Two Flower Gardens in a Farmstead in the Heart of the Auge Region

Two simple, spirited flower gardens, also designed by Louis Benech, greet one at the property called La Plesse. They are in perfect harmony with the landscape and with the beauty and tradition of the buildings as well as with their function, for this is a working farm. These gardens are both cozy and "cottagy," attached to the manor house and yet open to the countryside.

Is this a road or a sunken passageway which winds endlessly between the farmland hedges? A deer passes by. We are miles from anywhere, in the heart of deepest Normandy in the Auge region. This is real country—undulating, cheerful, and unspoiled. The road changes into a well-kept fine gravel path, and then there it is: the Manoir de La Plesse, its brick and sculpted half-timbering dating from the fifteenth century, accompanied by its bread oven, outbuildings, cider press and distillery, cart barn, stables, and of course its flower gardens.

The *jardin de curé* (cottage-style garden) follows the gentle, natural grade of the meadow down towards the pastures and a lake. The plantings are structured around a central axis that runs parallel to the slope, the perspective punctuated by box globes. From it, perpendicular grassy paths divide the beds into rectangles in the style of kitchen gardens. They are planted with a few vegetables and quantities of flowers chosen in all simplicity: dahlias, asters, dame's violet—sometimes known as sweet rocket (*Hesperis matronalis*), sedum (or stonecrop), lady's mantle (*Alchemilla mollis*), marguerites, cosmos, sweet peas, rudbeckia, and solidasters. At the highest level, these flowerbeds terminate in espaliered pear trees interspersed with holly cubes, which together form the sides of a staircase. At their feet 'Pink Panda' strawberry plants are used as groundcover. At the lowest extremity the beds are planted with apple trees pruned into goblet shapes. An herb garden borders the manor house near the kitchen, between the slate wall and a hedge of frothy, bright pink rosebushes propagated by cuttings. The garden is planted

In this same richly colored garden, created by Louis Benech, the sedum in the foreground flowers in the autumn. Behind it, lady's mantle (Alchemilla mollis) with its yellow froth and the blue fleabane (erigeron) flower at the end of the spring, just after the tall delphiniums which can be distinguished in the background.

with thyme, rosemary, sage, tarragon, chives, and fennel.

Near the manor the White Garden is laid out on a smooth terrace, which is slightly cambered for greater softness and appeal. It is backed by a dark yew hedge punctuated by trellises trained with a 'Madame Alfred Carrière' climbing rose and a 'Madame Lecoultre' clematis. Here Louis Benech assembled slightly off-white flowers. Pearly, tinted with mauve or pink, or almost green, they are much prettier than flowers that are stark white. He combined them with grayish-green foliage in harmony with the blue-green woodwork of the manor house. One can distinguish the big ivory corollas of the poppy *Papaver* 'Perry's White'; the large white flowers and gray foliage of the California poppy, *Romneya coulteri*; the tree peony, *Paeonia suffruticosa alba*; herbaceous peonies such as *Paeonia candidissima*; the 'Couronnes Virginales' Japanese anemones; 'White Wave' or 'Annabelle' hydrangeas, which turn green at the end of the summer; and all kinds of elegant roses. The English 'Winchester Cathedral' rose is a real beauty with its loose double flowers tinged with pink and fawn. 'Fair Bianca', another rose obtained by David Austin, has denser, fully double flowers and eyes like green buttons. Also on view is 'Little White Pet', a small rosebush with white flowers and pink buds. Among the blue-green foliage is the beautiful *Geranium renardii* with its matte, velvety, sage-green leaves and its purple-veined white flowers; the magnificent embossed foliage of the hosta *Sieboldiana glauca*; and also the common rue (*Ruta graveolens*). One observes gramineae such as blue oat grass (*Avena sempervirens*), blue fescue (*Festuca glauca*) and the blue-green foliage of lyme grass (*Leymus arenarius*). In the adjacent meadow, the gray tops of a double row of weeping pear trees (*Pyrus salicifolia* 'Pendula') with their silver willow leaves, should soon emerge over the top of the yew hedges.

The garden at La Plesse is like a smile in which one discerns good humor, vivacity, and a gentle way of life. It is reminiscent of the traditional Norman farmstead gardens situated close to the house and the animals. And animals there are, for white cows can be seen drinking from the ponds. Louis Benech replaced a hedge which impeded the view by a ha-ha, so now the beauty of the landscape can be fully appreciated. It is a garden that is easy to live with and in which it is equally pleasant to stroll, pick a fruit, or work. It is not a demanding garden and exists for pure enjoyment.

The Roses and Fragrances of the Prieuré Saint-Michel

A few hills away, near Vimoutiers in the Auge region, one should not miss a visit to the Prieuré Saint-Michel to savor the perfume of the roses, preferably at the end of June and if possible in the evening or, failing that, at midday, which are the privileged times when the fragrances are most pungent.

The buildings disposed around the courtyard were built between the thirteenth and eighteenth centuries. The present owners, Monsieur and Madame Chahine, organize exhibitions and conferences. They also welcome guests via the associations "Bienvenue au Château" and "Château Accueil." Today the priory boasts an herb garden, a *potager* (or kitchen garden), a water garden, a beautiful iris garden, and a rose garden, all open to the public.

The rose garden was designed in October 1989 by Louis Benech and planted with roses from the famed Delbard nurseries. Henri Delbard has given some wonderful conferences there on the subject of perfumes.

The rose garden was designed to be the setting for a fragrant stroll; its carefully adorned "rooms" evoke a series of surprises and delights. Louis Benech wanted it to be enclosed by hedges but nevertheless open to the countryside—both intimate and airy, but without drafts. The rose garden is divided into larger and smaller compartments. They are planted with rosebushes grouped by color and by fragrance, so that the visitor proceeds from one olfactory landscape to another. The geometric design is symmetrically disposed around two perpendicular axes: a path and a multilevel waterway which cross each other in a hollow.

The itinerary begins with a white garden surrounded by tree-covered walks and composed of four squares planted with supple clumps of rosebushes. One can distinguish 'Grand Nord', 'Candeur', and the English

At the Manoir de La Plesse, floral art is cultivated. The 'Gruss an Aachen' rose is perfect for decorating the manor house. Its large, fragrant flowers, which resemble Old Garden roses, are vigorous and stay fresh a long time.

The monastery garden at the Prieuré Saint-Michel contains traditional plants. One can find Old Garden roses such as Rosa gallica 'Versicolor' (also called 'Mundi'), which was introduced in 1583 by Clusius. This rose belongs to the same family as R. gallica var. officinalis or 'Apothecary's Rose', which was cultivated for its astringent properties and for perfume distillation, its blooms being very fragrant (facing page).

*In the Prieuré
garden, the main axis of
the rose garden crosses
white, pink, and yellow
garden rooms. Here the
pink garden is planted
with 'Milrose' and
'Bordure rose' bushes
(above). 'Ballerina' is a
musk rose hybrid which
was obtained in
England in 1937. A
profusion of single
blooms flowers from
June until autumn
(below).*

'Graham Thomas' and 'Fair Bianca' roses cultivated by David Austin.

One then proceeds to the pink garden enclosed by yews, composed of six squares planted with a mixture of 'Bordure Rose', 'Centenaire de Lourdes', 'Queen Elizabeth', 'Milrose', and 'Heritage' rosebushes.

The last garden in one's line of vision is yellow. It features an ornamental lake in the shape of a cross bordered by four squares planted with 'Bordure d'Or' rosebushes, softened by 'Fair Bianca' and 'Bordure de nacre'.

The water's cascade down from another source draws one's eye until one catches a glimpse of another garden. This one is pink and purple and enclosed by copper beeches. Purple berberis (commonly known as barberry) forms cushions on the banks of the lake, where one would be tempted to kneel down if it weren't for the thorns. Clipped purple smoke trees (*Cotinus coggygria*) stand as door frames. The combination of these three textures of purple foliage clipped and used in a classic yet unexpected fashion creates a tapestry effect which enhances this garden and sets off the 'Tobago', 'Madame Delbard', and 'Abraham Darby' roses. Upon leaving, one discovers exuberant climbing roses trained along cords.

The hedges are pruned so as to retain the fragrances without impeding the view over the countryside. "In this garden it is necessary to open one's mind, one's senses, and one's heart," explains Henri Delbard.

One must also savor the countless perfumes of the roses, each one of which can be analyzed and deconstructed. A rose may have a floral, fruity, woody, or spicy fragrance. It can smell of lily-of-the-valley, lilac, carnation, peach, or moss.

Take the 'Graham Thomas' rose with its deep, rich, yellow flowers tinted with apricot. It doesn't smell like a rose, but rather of autumn: moss, wood, mushrooms, and ferns. It is an underwood rose and its perfume is green and fresh. As to 'Fair Bianca', its flowers resemble those of Old Garden roses. They are pure white and fully double. They smell of aniseed, vanilla, hyacinth, and daffodils. Their delectable perfume is strong, persistent, and unforgettable.

At the Prieuré Saint-Michel the rosebushes are grouped by variety and in sufficient quantity to reveal their personalities. The color harmonies and fragrances are at their ultimate in the carefully designed and maintained structure, which serves both as protection and setting for the spectacular arrays of blooms.

Flowers Chosen
to Bloom
for a Single Month

In order to visit the gardens of Pontrancart one must leave the Auge and cross into the Seine-Maritime department, nearing the town of Dieppe.

Every year, between 15 August and 15 September, a veritable horticultural spectacle is played out in the flower garden of the Château du Pontrancart. All the buds burst into flower at the same time. This is the result of meticulous, organized, and passionate work with perennial and annual plants, skillfully chosen and cultivated.

plants from the wind and the spray, but the occasional slight breeze sometimes makes them reel. Since the hedges remain immobile, the sight is all the more beautiful.

This garden dates from the thirties, when the current owner's father purchased the property. He decided to make a flower garden where a *potager* no doubt once existed. He planted hedges, which he kept low. He followed the advice of his friend Miss Lloyd Jones, the English amateur landscape gardener, concerning the planting of the flowerbeds. He replaced the gravel paths with grassy ones. Then the war came and the gardeners were mobilized. The garden was neglected and discouragement set in. In the meantime, however, the hedges grew and this had the effect of distinctly improving

*At
Pontrancart, to mark
the passage from one
colored garden room to
another, Russell Page
advised planting
roundabouts of white
'Iceberg' roses.*

From a distance the garden resembles a labyrinth, due to the dense, static yew hedgerows which partition off the space. These walls of greenery delimit the compartments, each of which is devoted to a color theme. There is a red, a yellow, and a blue garden in which the plants illustrate the complete color spectrum, painting the tones and half tones with great finesse. The colors are never glaring, the combinations create modulations, and the scenes are dazzling. This is no doubt due to the abundance of the plants, which are all the same placed with a great deal of lightness and delicacy and never clash. They are in perfect health and seem invulnerable. The interventions of the gardeners go unnoticed and yet they watch over the beauty all the year round. The hedges protect the

the place. For instead of seeing the garden at a glance, one would make one discovery after another when passing from one compartment to another, prolonging the exploration and lending it far more charm. Since then, the composition of the flowerbeds has never ceased to improve. The best French and foreign seed catalogues are read each year so that innovations might be found. New associations are tried out, experimentally at first. Progress is made in the choice of color, texture, and bearing. All this is carried out with much enthusiasm and discipline.

From the Louis XIII château one has a view over the whole garden. The banks of the moat are planted with pink-toned flowers to create a transition—pink Japanese anemones, stonecrop (*Sedum* 'Autumn Joys'), and purple berberis to match the bricks. One follows a multicolored platform backed up against the wall of the former kitchen garden and enters the flower labyrinth. The blue garden was its creator's favorite. It is a blue and silver masterpiece. The azure tints are represented by the delicate trembling blue flowers of meadow rue (*Thalictrum dipterocarpum*), round-headed agapanthus, lavender-spired perovskia, and, in all simplicity, by ageratum (known as floss flowers) and delphiniums. Cosmos, spider flowers, and valerian provide a white accompaniment. Cineraria and *Stachys lanata* (commonly known as bunnies' ears or lamb's tongue), form the silver links. Then one changes compartment and color range. Yellows, reds, pinks, and lime greens succeed each other with the same perfection and

retarded. They are well-nurtured. Faded blooms are immediately removed. This is tedious work but it permits new flowers to bloom very quickly. Certain perennials which flower at the right moment are treated as annuals and replanted every year. The plants here do not have time to grow old. They are always stunning and they all meet at the same moment, at the height of their beauty.

A Showcase Garden Near Varengeville

Isabel Canovas has created a garden which is always of impeccable appearance. It is an

always in profusion and delicacy. Russell Page, who visited the garden, contributed an astute method of passing from one color theme to another without creating a clash. To soften the intersection of a multicolored and a yellow walk, he suggested composing a white roundabout with 'Iceberg' roses. For white systematically unites everything.

A secret garden was recently created in this same flower labyrinth, tucked behind the yew partitions. It is planted with little bushes and dwarf conifers, cryptomeria, variegated and green hollies, golden mint, green santolina, and chartreuse-colored euphorbia or milkweed. This variegated and golden garden is of a wilder nature, but is very luminous and soft.

At Pontrancart all the flowers are in perfect health even if the flowerings are forced or

arrangement of precious flowers dominated by whorled compact roses (notably the Old Garden roses), abetted by simple flora such as the fragile apple blossom, which all too soon blows away in the wind.

All the corollas unfurl around a slate, brick, and flint house named "L'Ancien Presbytère," which Mme. Canovas acquired about twenty years ago. At that time the garden was invaded by wild grasses. First she planted a lawn and then lindens, poplars, box, and yews. And then came the rosebushes.

The designer has an inborn sense of detailed overall planning. Everything here is precious and orderly. This garden is in fact quite an exploit, considering the wind and the spray tossed off from the nearby sea. One is quite unaware of these elements, however,

The flower maze once again: a pink and red flowerbed combines dahlias, sedum, cosmos, and castor oil plants. The flowers are varied, abundant, supple, and very spruce.

because this garden of refined and sophisticated plants is protected by walls, sturdy rows of linden trees, hedges that line and protect the compartments, and by other examples of impeccably trimmed architectural vegetation both unchanging and invulnerable. Box borders and clipped yews in the shape of cones, pyramids, and embankments, backed up against the walls, form the enclosures for this garden. This dense evergreen vegetation punctuates and divides up the spaces occupied predominantly by standard rose trees, among which one can distinguish a 'Centenaire de Lourdes' and a 'Madame Meilland' scornfully vying with a 'Grand Siècle' and a 'Jardin de Bagatelle'. For Isabel Canovas looks for roses which above all are both beautiful and fragrant. She is increasingly interested by Old Garden roses, and to make the transition has tried out David Austin English roses. These give her entire satisfaction, especially the white 'Fair Bianca' or the apricot-colored flowers of an 'Abraham Darby', which are her favorites. Scattered among the roses one finds perennials such as columbines, lupins, bellflowers, and carefully tutored delphiniums, as well as heavenly blue irises.

Isabel Canovas is a nature lover. She listens to and draws inspiration from it. She follows its

demands, and attempts to penetrate its mysteries. For example, she is interested by the influence of the moon. If the boxwoods are sparse, she will have them clipped during a waxing moon, whereas the yews, which need to keep their shape even if they need to be bushier, will be clipped during a waning moon.

The designer employs nature in her fashion collections. One year she created ballerina pumps with a dandelion flowering on the left foot, whereas sweet peas climbed up the heels of her court shoes and scattered seeds adorned one gloved hand. Flowers enhanced shawls and hats. Isabel Canovas dreams up these botanical fantasies in Paris on her return from weekends spent in Normandy.

A Creation
by Gilles Clément
in the Vexin

The landscape architect Gilles Clément, cocreator of the spectacular Citroën Park in Paris, knows how to blend flowers and colors perfectly. He also knows how to show them off to their best advantage by setting them against

a foliage backdrop of scrupulously trimmed hedges, which partition and protect them and contrast with their hazy, filmy shapes.

The house is of recent construction and walls enclose the garden. It is planted on the site of a former kitchen garden, where stands a magnificent nineteenth-century glass and wrought iron greenhouse. This rare structure has been lovingly restored. Gilles Clément planned the new garden around the greenhouse, consciously configuring the design so that the building's presence is discreet rather than dominating. It is partially hidden behind a hedge but the rooftop, which is just visible, attracts one's curiosity.

The garden, surrounded by beeches, is divided into rectangular chambers of greenery. The first garden is multicolored and the beds contain clumps of ligularia with its rich round foliage, perennial geraniums, and the deeper cut foliage of sedum. The beds are also planted with Japanese rosebushes, several pale yellow, single-flowered 'Golden Wing' roses, abelia (whose pale pink flowers are precious at the end of the summer), and with nandina, whose light delicate foliage takes on beautiful colors in the autumn. All the colors are understated and the flowers last throughout the summer months.

The second garden is yellow and silver. One can distinguish the single flowers of hugonis roses which bloom in May, 'Golden Wings' roses, achillea, rudbeckia, golden chamomile, orange hemerocallis, daylilies, and gray santolina.

The third garden is blue and white and very refined. Campanula, veronica, and sages accompany 'Iceberg' roses, the magnificent pink and white blooms of the elegant arching shrub rose 'Nevada', and several Japanese snowball trees (*Vibernum plicatum* 'Mariesii'). From here one has a better view of the greenhouse, which is in a line with the blue and white garden and is itself painted white. Formerly it contained apricot and fig trees. An arched grapevine, its roots outside the building, grows inside and produces good quantities of fruit.

Close by, one side of the house is enhanced by the large, pale yellow eglantine blooms of 'Mermaid' roses commingling with the white flowers of a 'Marie Boisselet' clematis and with honeysuckle, while at their feet grow

domes of Mexican orange blossom (*Choisya ternata*).

The walls on the other side of the house are covered with beautiful foliage. A crimson glory vine (*Vitis coignetiae*), a climbing hydrangea (*H. petiolaris*), the gray-green leaves of plume poppies (*Macleaya cordata*), nandinas, and the glossy leaves of a *Viburnum davidii* create an impression of profusion which is both welcoming and refreshing. All these plants blend perfectly together, just as if they had always been there.

Monet in Giverny: the Work of an Artist-Gardener

Claude Monet settled in Giverny, near Vernon, because he was attracted by the softness of the landscape and the beauty of the light; by the hills, orchards, and poplars; and the meanders of the river Seine. Enchanting too were the village and its houses stretching along the valley of the Epte river, most particularly one long pink and green house overlooking a large walled orchard. Here he made a very colorful flower garden. From 1883 he worked constantly in this enclosure, which he composed exactly like a picture, or then again perhaps he composed his pictures like a garden. Whatever the case, gardening fever gripped him as strongly as did painting, to the point that the two seemed to merge. Furthermore, he frequented artists and gardeners: Gustave Caillebotte, who in fact was both, as well as art critics Octave Mirbeau and Georges Truffaut.

First he dealt with the front garden. Here in the Clos Normand he created a *jardin de curé* of a regular design. In front of the house he imagined a central axis from which flowerbeds radiate, divided by a network of paths. Once the design was completed he set about the plantings. He kept the yews in front of the house, and gradually replaced the old fruit trees with Japanese flowering cherry and apple trees. The flowerbeds were planted with a profusion of bulbs, annuals, biennials, and perennials. He also installed trellises for climbing roses and clematis and punctuated the garden with standard rose trees. The contrast between the simplicity of the design and the

Octave Mirbeau, who visited Giverny in Monet's day, aptly describes La Grande Allée: *"It is summertime. Dazzling masses of myriad-toned nasturtiums and saffron-colored eschscholzias spill over the sandy walk on either side. The unbelievable magic of the poppies billows over the vast parterres, covering the faded irises. An extraordinary mixture of colors, a combat of pale tones, a radiant and musical profusion of white, pink, yellow, and mauve hues, an incredible succession of pale flesh-colored tones, on which orange shadows explode, gleaming brass fanfares, blazing blood reds; the violet tones frolic and the blackish purples are licked by the flames." Here, a cascade of flowers in July, those of the 'Excelsa' rose, which is unscented and very vigorous (above and center).*

exuberance of the flowers in a multitude of colors and varieties is lovely.

Obviously Monet was fascinated by the play of color in flowers. He knew how to use it in all its complexity. He planted flowers in clumps or individually. He favored lavender blue, pure white, soft pink, bright red, violet, and pale yellow. He always wanted the scenes near the house to tone in with the colors of the walls, so in spring these parterres display pink and red tulips underplanted with double daisies (*Bellis perennis*).

The best times of year for this garden, which is open to the public, are the end of May and mid-September. In May the lavender blue *Iris × germanica* are in bloom and they are magnificent. They are accompanied by fragrant orange-toned wallflowers (*Cheiranthus cheiri*), or the equally perfumed dame's violet or sweet rocket (*Hesperis matronalis*), and in the mauve color range by herbaceous peonies, *Aquilegia vulgaris* columbines (known as granny's bonnets), and also by bright red oriental poppies (*Papaver orientale*).

In September, La Grande Allée is magnificent. The trellises are blanketed under remontant roses and the path is inundated with garden nasturtiums, sometimes known as Indian cress (*Tropaeolum majus*). On each side, dahlias, mauve asters and golden yellow sunflowers (*Helianthus multiflorus*) offer abundant sprays.

On the whole Monet liked all sorts of plants. He took great care in choosing them. "I have at last managed to find wallflowers," he wrote to his wife, ". . . several other packets will arrive in Vernon which will need to be opened with care. They contain perennials and passion flowers for the temperate greenhouse, as well as some curious little nasturtiums."

He did not care for variegated plants, considering them too far removed from the natural species. He liked simple flowers and wild plants like verbascum (commonly known as mullein), which he allowed to self-sow. Nevertheless some two-toned flowers—like certain irises—found favor with him, as did shaded flowers like peonies, which he particularly appreciated and sometimes procured from English nurseries. He tried out all sorts of seeds and amused himself with horticultural experiments. Even if he did employ five gardeners, Monet was an inveterate and authentic artist-gardener.

Monet was fascinated by his garden. He was a real plantsman. Here is what he wrote to his head gardener: "From the 15th to the 25th, put the budding dahlias on a hotbed; make cuttings from those that come out. Don't forget the lily bulbs. If the Japanese peonies arrive and the weather permits, plant them on-site straight away, but be careful to protect the buds at first from cold temperatures or hot sun. Do the pruning: not too long for the roses, apart from the thorny varieties." Monet's garden was restored in the 1980s and it offers an uninterrupted succession of flowerings from spring to autumn. The metal trellises which support climbing roses and clematis have been reinstated (facing page).

A Garden of the Five Senses in Thury-Harcourt

At Thury-Harcourt, near Caen, the duchesse d'Harcourt herself tends the flower garden, which was created by her husband. She removes the faded flowers and does the weeding accompanied by her dog (center). A close-up of a multicolored scene composed of red dahlias, mauve floss flowers (ageratum), and yellow evening primroses (oenothera, below).

The duc and duchesse d'Harcourt love flowers; indeed the duc is the author of a celebrated work entitled *Des Jardins Heureux*. It radiates much humility and love of the natural world, as well as true wisdom. From this book one learns how to compose a garden and how to obtain results which respect nature.

At Thury-Harcourt in the Calvados county, the duc created a flower garden to help forget the ruins of the château destroyed during the Second World War. Part of an extensive park that is open to the public, the garden is the embodiment of the principles evoked in his publication.

It is a studied garden whose hidden meaning needs to be deciphered. The duc's explanations appear to be quite simple. "In the field of art," he writes, "the maximum effect is always obtained with minimum means." However, behind this simplicity many ideas are concealed, in virtue of the following principle: "a beautiful garden must satisfy the demands of our senses, our intelligence and our spirit." The duc d'Harcourt developed a theme in

depth without becoming distracted by other temptations: "unity in composition is essential," he specifies. The design centers around two perpendicular axes. "The axis of a garden is the invisible line around which a fragment of landscape is laid out." The flower borders form simple rectangles and enclose vast lawns. Indeed "empty space is perhaps the most important element in parks and gardens. It is an expression of the invisible, a mysterious call, a pole around which everything is designed. It is the equivalent of silence, which, one must never forget, is one of the components of eloquence."

It should be noted that the dimensions of the rectangles are not arbitrary. They are particularly harmonious, for the duc applied the rule of the golden section used by the Greeks, which results in rectangles with dimensions of 1×1.62 meters. He called upon his artistic talents in selecting the colors, and those of a musician in orchestrating the mixed borders. The beauty of the garden appeals to the intellect because it is based upon the harmonies of geometry. But it also delights the senses, since it engages sight, hearing, the sense of smell, and touch. Sight is self-explanatory. Hearing because all this vegetation

The duc d'Harcourt chose a simple design. He uncoiled a garland of flowers on a green carpet and gave it the geometric forms characteristic of gardens à la française (facing page).

The same concern for color harmony at Thury-Harcourt: pink dahlias and similarly colored penstemon, whose tubular flowers on spindly stems stand out against the feathery cosmos foliage (facing page).

A few of the flowers which adorn the gardens at Thury-Harcourt. The malopes (above left) are annuals which flower all summer from June to September and are self-sowing. Salpiglossis sinuata with their velvety, veined petals (above right) originate from Chile; they exist in crimson, scarlet, yellow, and lavender-blue and flower between July and September. Hibiscus syriacus 'Oiseau Bleu' punctuate the garland as well as the classic geometric motif at the intersection of the two main axes (below left). Petunias obtained from seeds fill the gaps (below right).

is a refuge for birds. One's sense of smell because of the fragrance of these plants, and finally touch thanks to the feel of the soft green carpet of grassy walkways underfoot.

As for the plantings, the duc d'Harcourt listened respectfully to the demands of nature, without forcing it. He wanted to "fulfill its secret wishes." He knew the type of soil and the climate with its sunshine and rainfall. Then he made his choice, retaining only plants which would thrive there. Amongst the annuals he chose *Salvia farinacea*, cosmos, cleomes

(commonly known as spider flowers), and zinnias. For the perennials he chose phlox, monarda or bergamot, nepetas, and shrubs like hibiscus and rosebushes. All these flowers succeed one another from the beginning of the summer until the first frosts.

The result is simple, pure, and tranquil. The duc wrote: "A garden which does not inspire serenity does not fulfill its role, since what we are searching for when in contact with a particularly beautiful expression of nature is a sensation of peace and restfulness."

A Profusion of Flowers
in the Gardens and Groves
of Vandrimare

The flower gardens at Vandrimare near Fleury-sur-Andelle, not far from Rouen, are as thoughtfully planned as those found at Thury-Harcourt.

They transmit a message which has to be deciphered on two levels: aesthetic and philosophical. They are the result of a perfect complicity between a gifted landscape architect, Clotilde Duvoux-Bouchayer, and two cultured gardeners, Monsieur and Madame de La Conté.

The Vandrimare gardens are laid out around a white château, whose façade is punctuated by numerous windows. It was built in the seventeenth century and the gardens' classic design also dates from that period. Subsequently they were partially reconfigured in the English style. Since 1989, Monsieur and Madame de La Conté have introduced many new ideas. They created a flower and hedge garden in the former kitchen garden: a place for contemplation. Along the wall where fruit trees were trained, they planted the Tactile Garden. Farther along, the

Cloister Garden invites the visitor to reflect while savoring the fragrances. Next comes the Berry Garden for tasting. Then the labyrinth must be negotiated, which requires reasoning. Finally one reaches the recently planted enclosed Grove Garden, which is amusing, astonishing, and attractive due to its complexity and promise of future beauty. The visit does not end there as other theme gardens are constantly being created.

Let us recapitulate and appreciate them one by one. The flower garden is partitioned by yew hedges in increasing heights from the center outwards. The parterres are mainly planted with perennials and bulbs grouped by color, the only concession to symmetry being their distribution around a central walk. Starting from the center one discovers in turn flowerbeds in white, lime green, pale and deep yellow, soft orange, and almost black tones. These are followed by pale pink and silver, deep pink, lilac and purple, soft blue and silver, mid-blue and violet. They satisfy all desires of plants and colors and the progression of the various compartments is very lovely. One seeks out the hues that one anticipates in advance. One wants to approach the plants closely, so as to observe their corollas and

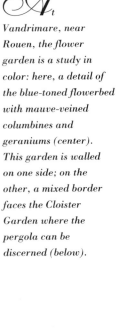

At Vandrimare, near Rouen, the flower garden is a study in color: here, a detail of the blue-toned flowerbed with mauve-veined columbines and geraniums (center). This garden is walled on one side; on the other, a mixed border faces the Cloister Garden where the pergola can be discerned (below).

foliage in detail. The color harmonies and shadings are very studied and intricate.

A change of scene. Now that the sense of sight has been gratified, one proceeds to the sense of touch. A long border stands against a former kitchen garden wall. It bristles with prickers, spikes, and thorns. One can distinguish the *Carlina acanthifolia* thistle; acanthus; the long, red translucid thorns of a pteracantha rose; all kinds of eryngium or sea holly; the tall silver *Onopordum arabicum* thistles; mahonia; and blackberry brambles (such as the *Rubus thibetanus* whose silver and blue branches are armed with numerous thorns). After running this gauntlet, which extends all the way down the path, a lovely green lawn awaits. It is time for a rest.

The Cloister Garden, next on the itinerary, is very recent. This is another important moment. The garden is sheltered, intimate, and secret. It is floral, romantic, and fragrant. An encircling pergola is smothered in all kinds of creepers such as wisteria, vines, and roses (such as 'Dorothy Perkins', 'Gloire de Dijon', 'Zephrine Drouin', 'Adelaide d'Orléans', and many more). The pergola is barely visible under all these fragrant flowers. It is like a magical perfume

garden, especially in June. Inside, there is an array in gray, purple, and green tones of medieval inspiration. Here slow-growing vegetation is clipped (to give the illusion of indifference to the passage of time) and is evergreen (to simulate eternity). In this haven, sage, box, rue, and rosemary are combined with mint, chamomile, savory, and oregano.

The Berry Garden is a gourmet's opportunity to taste at a stroll. The trees and shrubs are planted in a seemingly random fashion. One can distinguish apricot, almond, fig, hazelnut, and walnut trees. There are also all sorts of unexpected varieties such as amelanchier (commonly known as juneberries), arbutus, aronia or chokeberries, pomegranate trees, and raisin-trees (*Hovenia dulcis*).

The labyrinth is planted with hornbeams, which makes it less fearsome than those with dark evergreen yews. Two secret compartments hide within. Its design is irregular, disconcerting, but above all amusing.

A shady walk leads to the enclosed Grove Garden or the Perpetual Motion Grove, which encourages the viewer to meditate about time. Each floral compartment was inspired by a particular time of the day. One enters in turn the morning grove, the afternoon, the tea-time, and

At Vandrimare, violet Campanula glomerata flower in the company of a white variety, C. persicifolia 'Alba' (center). The multicolored flower garden is structured by yew hedges. Farther on, the central axis leads to the Cloister Garden (below).

In the Jardins d'Angélique, near Rouen, informally designed flowerbeds are planted with shrubs, mainly composed of rosebushes and perennials (center). One of the masterpieces of the extraordinary rose collection here are the musk rose (Rosa moschata) hybrids, so named because of their musky perfume. They have a delicate, graceful bearing (facing page).

evening groves. In each of them the flowers are grouped by level and change with the seasons. They bloom and they fade, replacing each other constantly, thus illustrating perpetual motion, which requires a very skillful orchestration of the flowerings.

One can also visit the water garden, the restored orangery, the greenhouse, and then proceed as far as the clay and straw mortar dovecote with its tiled roof, the bakery (also made of clay and straw and half-timbering), the sheepfold, the dairy, and the cart barn. All are typically Norman buildings raised with traditional materials.

Vandrimare will continue to surprise its visitors for many a day. It is a place for reflection, entertainment, and enrichment.

much influenced by the local Vasterival and Bois des Moutiers, as well as by two gardens in the south of England: Mottisfont and the enclosed garden at Wakehurst. The garden belonging to the rose specialist André Eve in Pithiviers, which combines roses, shrubs, and perennials, was also particularly influential.

By following the grassy paths which border the hazy contours of the flowerbeds in front of the manor house, one can admire six hundred rosebushes of 380 different varieties. This is proof enough that the collection has already made considerable headway. The owners' ambition is to cultivate vast quantities of roses and to rehabilitate forgotten varieties such as 'Jeanne d'Arc' and 'Robert le Diable', two typically Norman roses. They would be regrouped

The Six Hundred Rosebushes in the Jardins d'Angélique

The Jardins d'Angélique, not far away in Montmain, near Rouen, is not to be missed. It is a rose garden which is feminine, delicate, and fragrant. Beautiful all the year round, the site is particularly magnificent at the beginning of summer when the roses are in bloom. The garden has been named after the daughter of Monsieur and Madame Lebellegard.

At the outset the owners of this garden knew nothing about plants, nor how to cultivate them. However, little by little, gardening fever took hold. They learned as they went along and by visiting other gardens. They were

by breeder, so there would be a Parmentier, a Vibert, and an Oger Garden. There would also be a species rose garden to illustrate what nature had to offer at the outset.

The collection now includes numerous Old Garden roses, more recently obtained specimens, and especially remontant roses to multiply the flowerings—which are preceded by spring bulbs and followed by beautiful autumn colors.

The flowerbeds contain plants which blend well with roses: blue nepetas or catmint, campanulas, delphiniums, lilies, alliums, foxgloves, gramineae, *Salvia sclarea*, gray artemisia (or wormwood), and geraniums. The garden is deliciously perfumed. The roses can be seen from a distance or close up. One can admire the richness of the colors, the beauty of the corollas, the elegance of the bearing, and the foliage.

All the rosebushes are treated with great imagination and any pretext is good for training them in various ways. Here a rambler is seen growing up a fruit tree (following pages).

One of the crowning glories of this garden is the 'Salet' rose, which was obtained in 1854, a rose-bush whose buds are timidly covered in green moss. The blooms are pink, fully double, and fragrant and they flower until the end of summer. The 'Comte de Chambord', a remontant Portland rose obtained in 1860, is a great beauty with its fragrant, fully double lilac-tinted pink flowers in quartered rosette form. In a different, more orange-ish tone, 'Buff Beauty' spreads its lovely, wide, supple branches and is smothered with clusters of large fully double fragrant flowers all through summer.

In the Jardins d'Angélique the roses are on stage. It is a place where one can draw inspiration, glean ideas, learn about roses, and share a mutual passion.

Flowers From All Over the World at the Clos du Coudray

The Clos du Coudray, a floral park in the Caux region near Etaimpuis, was opened to the public in 1993. It was created by Jean Le Bret, who has been working constantly in this garden for nearly fifteen years. He is a well-informed and devoted botanist. He has collected more than five thousand species and varieties of plants from all corners of the world: from the Himalayas, Australia, Japan, the Andes cordillera, and from all the temperate zones.

The garden borders a stream and occasionally follows an upward slope. For the most part, the flowerbeds trace a meandering pattern, though some gardens are laid out along straighter lines or border the house. In the various gardens which constitute this large park, plants are grouped according to cultivation conditions, resulting in congregations like the Fern Garden, the Primula Garden, or the Condiment Garden. When the conditions are immaterial, the plants are grouped by color, for example the White Garden, the Yellow, or the Pink Garden. All these scenes are composed with the viewer's instruction in mind, so that one can draw inspiration, comprehend, examine, and learn. All the plants are labeled and one can usually find these rarities on sale in the nursery at the entrance to the park.

How did Jean Le Bret go about acclimatizing all these foreign plants? He was obliged to cheat in Normandy, to compose with the typically damp lowlands to create situations foreign to the soil and the climate—such as even

damper, almost marshy, flowerbeds, or at the opposite extreme, arid, rocky zones. If a newly introduced plant survives, flowers, and produces seeds, that is sufficient proof to him that it will thrive. Take primulas for example, notably the *P. flaccida*, originating from western China, with its gentian blue flowers and its chalky stems. It does best in peat that is light and loose. Here in Normandy the soil is damp, but also heavy and compact and air does not penetrate. Jean Le Bret therefore re-created here in the Clos du Coudray the necessary humid atmosphere and this primula is now a perennial, whereas elsewhere it is considered a biennial.

He has met with similar success with the famous blue poppy from the Himalayas,

Carefully Labeled Flowers in the Cotelle Family's Nursery Garden

Also in the Caux region, in the charming hamlet of Derchigny near Dieppe, a castle and a church steeple tower over Frédéric and Catherine Cotelle's garden, which is right next door to their nursery.

It is a typical cottage garden with densely sown plants growing in liberty as though they had been scattered in a very spontaneous fashion. It is a garden where one can admire the plants close up and savor the smallest details: the shape of a petal; the beauty of a corolla, a pistil, or a stamen; the elegance of a stem; or

Meconopsis betonicifolia, which has become self-sowing, which is extremely rare here.

The Clos du Coudray also possesses one of the richest private rock gardens. It is remarkable for its collection of primulas, penstemon, saxifraga, hostas, asters, phlox, dryopteris, and diascia.

Jean Le Bret created this floral park with two main objectives. He first wanted to prove to plant lovers that creating a garden is within everyone's reach, and to this end, he hopes his serves as encouragement. Second, he traveled around the globe in order to collect unusual vegetation so that he could make a world tour whenever he walked round his plantings. There is always something happening at the Clos du Coudray and the flowers never miss their cue to dazzle the eye.

the texture of the foliage. This is a garden with all sorts of exuberant but unpretentious mixed borders. It is laid out around a mossy roofed house with low windows, which also serves as the couple's office. It is half-timbered and trellised. The garden is enclosed and intimate, with narrow, winding, grassy paths.

One of these paths slopes gently between two flowerbeds, then veers away to lead to another, which serves as a "welcome" bouquet to the house. One proceeds alongside, notebook in hand, for all the plants are labeled. Towards the back of the house, a second garden is discovered. Its paths seem to get lost in the underwood, but of course they are prevented from such a fate by the fencing.

The garden is planted with shrubs, perennials, biennials, and bulbs. In general, these are simple plants which can withstand the capricious climate (which often belies the legendary mildness of the region). Prolific vegetation is used as groundcover to avoid weeds and facilitate upkeep. The owners have composed a garden that is easy to live with and beautiful all year round. They often planned it looking out of the windows to ensure a pleasant view from inside the house. In the nursery next door, the same varieties can be observed fully grown and are available for purchase.

The garden holds rosebushes, fragrant vibernum, generous phlomis, thorny mahonias, spindle trees, spiraea, and potentilla. Among the flowers should be noted the clumps of campanula, euphorbia, asters, and Japanese anemones. Also here are plenty of charm-

flamboyant tones in autumn with yellow, red, and orange chrysanthemums, ligularia, sunflowers (helianthus), bronze fennel, and 'Preziosa' hydrangeas.

Catherine Cotelle, who is a watercolorist, likes composing scenes and playing with colors. She plants beautiful "bouquets" and twice a week she comes back from the garden with great armfuls of flowers. She dares using unusual combinations like perennial geraniums and irises with the variegated foliage of daylilies (hemerocallis). So all year round she is able to appreciate the garden even when she is indoors. Today Frédéric and Catherine Cotelle have great projects concerning the land around the church and family château adjoining their house, in memory of their ancestor,

Catherine Cotelle painting in her garden among the catmint (Nepeta 'Six Hills Giant'), the roses, and the silver chard.

This plant with its unusually shaped, large, decorative leaves is a wild variety of senecio, a weed which has Catherine's permission to stay. Behind it flowers a Weigela praecox 'Variegata', which, according to the plant nursery catalogue, is "one of the most beautiful weigelas with green, silver, and pink foliage and bright pink flowers with pale pink hearts."

ing flowers traditionally found in cottage gardens such as primulas, violets, lupins, columbine, astrantia or masterwort, perennial geraniums, honesty, and dame's violets.

The colors of the garden follow those of the seasons, greenish yellow in the spring with the chartreuse green bracts of the various milkweeds such as *Euphorbia polychroma*, *E. characias* ssp. *wulfenii*, *E. amygdaloides* (wood spurge), *E. × martinii*, and *E. robbiae*. The garden takes on pastel shades in June with a white and blue predominance: *Campanula lactiflora*, the 'Six Hills Giants' nepeta catmint, and blue linaria, commonly known as toadflax. It brightens itself up in summer with yellow solidasters, *Geranium psilostermon*, *Phlomis samia*, phlox, and yellow *Silphium perfoliatum*. Finally the garden adorns itself in

Gabriel de Clieu, a Royal Navy officer, who had a passion for building and traveling and who planted the first coffee shrub in Martinique. They want to create a historical theme garden, to perpetuate the family's botanical traditions. The nursery will continue to stock cottage garden plants and in addition one will be able to purchase heritage specimens.

Flowers All Year Round in a Village Garden

The garden surrounding the Manoir d'Arthur is planted with perennials and shrubs and is beautiful all the year round, for the flowerings in the English-style mixed borders succeed each other without a break. The manor house was built in the Renaissance style in white stone from Caen. It is situated in Saint-Laurent de Condel, a village on the border of the plain of Caen and the Suisse Normande, not far from Thury-Harcourt.

This garden was created in 1975 by Monsieur and Madame Aubin, who had just purchased the manor. They are both landscape architects with degrees from the Ecole Normale Supérieure d'Horticulture in Versailles. On arrival they found no trace of garden, merely a very large bramble. They dealt with the courtyard first, then the terraces, and finally the banks along the stream.

In the courtyard rock crops out everywhere, which makes planting very difficult. The solution? Carpets of thyme cover the stones and bulbs snuggle in the cracks. In front of the house a very pretty scene of clipped box sets off the façade.

Farther away, near the farm buildings, a long flowerbed spreads out in a half circle. Additional floral banks rise in tiers on three levels overlooking the valley, the stream, and an ornamental lake.

The parade of blooms starts right off in January with the hellebores or Christmas roses, heather, and snowdrops, which

keep company with berry shrubs and beautiful barks. Hamamelis or witch hazel, *Viburnum × bodnantense*, mahonia, and daphne also flower in winter. They are followed by all kinds of bulbs and peonies, masses of brightly colored perennial geraniums and delphiniums, not to mention all the less spectacular spring flowers. Then come the hemerocalles, agapanthus, and phlox. In the late season, asters, crocosmia (otherwise known as montbretia), and chrysanthemums combine with the decorative raspberry-colored foliage of spindle trees, and with the berries to be found on the elders and *Symphoricarpos orbiculata* (known as coralberry or Indian currant).

All these plants are disposed in dense clumps which prevent weeds from proliferating. There is an exceptionally wide range of species, for not many years ago Madame Aubin ran a plant nursery and her garden served as a living catalogue for her clients.

Bordering the stream, the garden takes on a wilder appearance, rather as if it were nature who had sown the clumps of hydrangeas, montbretias, eupatorium, and the gigantic gunnera.

All the plants in the garden have now reached full maturity and the great sprays of flowers make a beautiful display.

Well-chosen perennials and shrubs provide a permanent décor for this all-year-round garden, created by Madame Aubin, surrounding the Manoir d'Arthur (center). At the foot of the Renaissance manor house, clipped plants framed by small box borders leave space for perennial plants (below).

A very pretty wrought iron gate, between walls of greenery, provides access to a garden room situated near the outbuildings (facing page).

At Bailleul in the Caux region, the Maison Normande and the garden form a single entity. The garden takes over the façade, enters the house, and can be admired from all the windows within (right and facing page). The cotoneaster turtles, with their heads of holly, are the work of the interior decorator Kim Moltzer, as in fact are all the contemporary gardens at Bailleul. When coming from the château one discovers, sitting on the lawn, the turtles, which announce the Maison Normande (below).

The Flowering Turtles in Bailleul

Three green turtles announce the proximity of the Maison Normande: cotoneaster turtles which are covered with masses of little white flowers in the spring, like a mantle of snow, while their holly heads remain very green. The Maison Normande is a mere stone's throw from the Renaissance château of Bailleul (see p. 81) in the Caux region and a park links these two edifices. This park was sometimes treated *à la française* and sometimes in the English style. Wide avenues and an axis oriented towards the village church steeple are bordered by majestic beeches planted on embankments. The current owner, interior decorator Kim Moltzer, relates that his wife's grandfather took the park's destiny in hand in the 1860s and replanted it; therefore these magnificent beeches which so enhance the décor date from that period.

Mr. Moltzer took pains to instill some life into the grounds by creating an herb garden and a labyrinth (see p. 81). He also created a garden around the Maison Normande, taking particular care with the shape and colors so as to be in perfect harmony with the mansion. The vegetation is nearly all clipped and is mostly ever-

green, except for a few shrub peonies, fuchsias, and rosebushes. It is variegated or in shades of green, purple, and gold and blends perfectly with the gingerbread tones of the half-timbering. There are purple berberis, pieris, silver or variegated eleagnus, *Viburnum tinus* (known as laurustinus), spindle trees, hollies, box, and yew trees. All these domes of vegetation are under strict control in a bed enclosed by low berberis hedgerows which border the house. Only the mahonias are allowed freedom of movement. The walls are covered by Virginia creeper, honeysuckle, pyracantha or firethorn, jasmine, and climbing roses like the 'Mermaid' rose with its strong stems, glistening foliage, large single primrose-yellow flowers and prominent stamens, all of which enhance the half-timbering. In autumn these warm tones melt into the softness of the garden and match the prodigious colors of the beeches which spread their elegant, nonchalant branches over the paths.

A Pink and Blue Garden in the Perche Region

At La Petite Rochelle, color harmony between house and garden also plays an important role, but the range is different. It is a

In the Perche region, the Jardin de Solvène, named after the granddaughter of the creator of this garden, Madame d'Andlau, is particularly radiant in the spring when the flowering cherries are in bloom (following pages).

pink and blue floral universe which tones in perfectly with the blue shutters, or to be more precise, gray-blue, which is the tradition in the Perche region. The flowers are pale or bright, in shades of fuchsia, lilac, and lavender.

La Petite Rochelle, which takes its name from one of the districts of the little Norman town in which the house is situated, is an artist's garden, for the proprietor, Madame d'Andlau, was a sculptor and engraver. She has an inborn sense of color, volume, perspective, and the vistas that can be obtained from certain angles. Her garden is like an Impressionist painting in an architectural frame constituted by walls, yew hedges, ivy, and the flowering *Prunus cerasifera* 'Pissardii', known as cherry plum. The flowers are disposed in little touches, they are light and supple and sway slightly in the wind.

When speaking of Madame d'Andlau, her uncle Prince Wolkonsky (himself an avid artist-gardener) explains that "she has a talent for ensuring color all the year round." This is quite an exploit, especially in autumn, when nature's palette shifts to flame-hued tones. In contrast, Madame d'Andlau's pink and blue flowers are mingled with foliage which turns to deep pink or purple. All shades of gold, old gold,

and lustrous bronze are banned. The asters, which have been chosen with great care over the years, blend in pleasantly with elegant cornus or dogwood, which turns to a garnet color and is itself interspersed with helenium, commonly known as sneezeweed.

The garden slopes down gently towards the valley of the Huisne river and the hills of the Perche region rise in the distance, forming a backdrop for the landscape. This garden is full of surprises. It is divided into compartments and one passes from each room to the next full of curiosity for the discoveries to come.

In front of the house, a pink and blue garden is laid out. It slopes down towards a labyrinth, the center of which is occupied by an ornamental lake. The plant profusion contrasts with a rigid yew hedge surmounted by topiary birds. Then one passes into Le Champ, where great quantities of trees and shrubs don pretty colors in the autumn: maples, liquidambars, crab apple trees (malus), and sorbus (known as mountain ash). Among the rarer species figure two varieties of nyssa: *N. sylvatica* or black gum and *N. sinensis*. Also on view are the 'Red Cascade' spindle tree (*Euonymus europaea*) with its red foliage and fruit, and the flamboyant *Perrotetia pendula*.

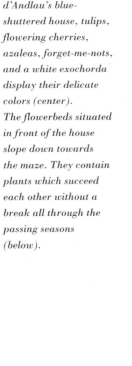

In the spring, in front of Madame d'Andlau's blue-shuttered house, tulips, flowering cherries, azaleas, forget-me-nots, and a white exochorda display their delicate colors (center). The flowerbeds situated in front of the house slope down towards the maze. They contain plants which succeed each other without a break all through the passing seasons (below).

pink and blue floral universe which tones in perfectly with the blue shutters, or to be more precise, gray-blue, which is the tradition in the Perche region. The flowers are pale or bright, in shades of fuchsia, lilac, and lavender.

La Petite Rochelle, which takes its name from one of the districts of the little Norman town in which the house is situated, is an artist's garden, for the proprietor, Madame d'Andlau, was a sculptor and engraver. She has an inborn sense of color, volume, perspective, and the vistas that can be obtained from certain angles. Her garden is like an Impressionist painting in an architectural frame constituted by walls, yew hedges, ivy, and the flowering *Prunus cerasifera* 'Pissardii', known as cherry plum. The flowers are disposed in little touches, they are light and supple and sway slightly in the wind.

When speaking of Madame d'Andlau, her uncle Prince Wolkonsky (himself an avid artist-gardener) explains that "she has a talent for ensuring color all the year round." This is quite an exploit, especially in autumn, when nature's palette shifts to flame-hued tones. In contrast, Madame d'Andlau's pink and blue flowers are mingled with foliage which turns to deep pink or purple. All shades of gold, old gold,

and lustrous bronze are banned. The asters, which have been chosen with great care over the years, blend in pleasantly with elegant cornus or dogwood, which turns to a garnet color and is itself interspersed with helenium, commonly known as sneezeweed.

The garden slopes down gently towards the valley of the Huisne river and the hills of the Perche region rise in the distance, forming a backdrop for the landscape. This garden is full of surprises. It is divided into compartments and one passes from each room to the next full of curiosity for the discoveries to come.

In front of the house, a pink and blue garden is laid out. It slopes down towards a labyrinth, the center of which is occupied by an ornamental lake. The plant profusion contrasts with a rigid yew hedge surmounted by topiary birds. Then one passes into Le Champ, where great quantities of trees and shrubs don pretty colors in the autumn: maples, liquidambars, crab apple trees (malus), and sorbus (known as mountain ash). Among the rarer species figure two varieties of nyssa: *N. sylvatica* or black gum and *N. sinensis*. Also on view are the 'Red Cascade' spindle tree (*Euonymus europaea*) with its red foliage and fruit, and the flamboyant *Perrotetia pendula*.

In the spring, in front of Madame d'Andlau's blue-shuttered house, tulips, flowering cherries, azaleas, forget-me-nots, and a white exochorda display their delicate colors (center). The flowerbeds situated in front of the house slope down towards the maze. They contain plants which succeed each other without a break all through the passing seasons (below).

pink and blue floral universe which tones in perfectly with the blue shutters, or to be more precise, gray-blue, which is the tradition in the Perche region. The flowers are pale or bright, in shades of fuchsia, lilac, and lavender.

La Petite Rochelle, which takes its name from one of the districts of the little Norman town in which the house is situated, is an artist's garden, for the proprietor, Madame d'Andlau, was a sculptor and engraver. She has an inborn sense of color, volume, perspective, and the vistas that can be obtained from certain angles. Her garden is like an Impressionist painting in an architectural frame constituted by walls, yew hedges, ivy, and the flowering *Prunus cerasifera* 'Pissardii', known as cherry plum. The flowers are disposed in little touches, they are light and supple and sway slightly in the wind.

When speaking of Madame d'Andlau, her uncle Prince Wolkonsky (himself an avid artist-gardener) explains that "she has a talent for ensuring color all the year round." This is quite an exploit, especially in autumn, when nature's palette shifts to flame-hued tones. In contrast, Madame d'Andlau's pink and blue flowers are mingled with foliage which turns to deep pink or purple. All shades of gold, old gold, and lustrous bronze are banned. The asters, which have been chosen with great care over the years, blend in pleasantly with elegant cornus or dogwood, which turns to a garnet color and is itself interspersed with helenium, commonly known as sneezeweed.

The garden slopes down gently towards the valley of the Huisne river and the hills of the Perche region rise in the distance, forming a backdrop for the landscape. This garden is full of surprises. It is divided into compartments and one passes from each room to the next full of curiosity for the discoveries to come.

In front of the house, a pink and blue garden is laid out. It slopes down towards a labyrinth, the center of which is occupied by an ornamental lake. The plant profusion contrasts with a rigid yew hedge surmounted by topiary birds. Then one passes into Le Champ, where great quantities of trees and shrubs don pretty colors in the autumn: maples, liquidambars, crab apple trees (malus), and sorbus (known as mountain ash). Among the rarer species figure two varieties of nyssa: *N. sylvatica* or black gum and *N. sinensis*. Also on view are the 'Red Cascade' spindle tree (*Euonymus europaea*) with its red foliage and fruit, and the flamboyant *Perrotetia pendula*.

In the spring, in front of Madame d'Andlau's blue-shuttered house, tulips, flowering cherries, azaleas, forget-me-nots, and a white exochorda display their delicate colors (center). The flowerbeds situated in front of the house slope down towards the maze. They contain plants which succeed each other without a break all through the passing seasons (below).

A purple hedge of flowering cherry plum *Prunus cerasifera* 'Pissardii' encloses the Italian Garden, which groups all the plants banned from the pink and blue garden, that is to say the cream, yellow, or orange flowers. It is a very structured arrangement. A central path bordered by low walls leads to a hexagonal space where white-flowering heather and helianthemum (rock roses) are interspersed with liriope (known as lilyturf)—a few touches of blue indeed have been allowed in.

When returning back up the slope, the pink and blue theme gradually takes over again. On the left there is an avenue of hornbeams underplanted with pink cyclamen and on the right a grotto which leads to another garden, then onward to an ornamental lake. Here and there are quantities of flowering cherry (prunus) growing among magnolias, which together are magnificent in the spring. The garden walls are trellised with a collection of clematis.

And so one returns towards the house and to the softness of the first garden, where in winter carpets of Christmas roses flower at the same time as a delicate Higan or rosebud cherry (*Prunus subhirtella* 'Autumnalis') and also, of course, daphne, which Madame d'Andlau collects.

She grows the rare, fragile varieties listed by the Conservatoire des Collections végétales spécialisées. They are followed by white narcissus *N.* 'Thalia', 'Jenny', and 'Mount Hood'; magnolias; pink 'Angélique' tulips; dogwood (including an elegant *Cornus nuttallii* 'Portlemouth' and the particularly beautiful pink-flowering *C. florida* 'Cherokee Chief'); as well as rhododendrons, campanulas, lilies, phlox, hydrangeas, Japanese anemones, and asters. Among the latter species figures a beautiful *Aster cordifolius* 'Ideal'. With its star-shaped flowers of a pretty blue, it perfectly complements the shutters.

From one year to the next, La Petite Rochelle stages a parade of flowers for the greater satisfaction of Madame d'Andlau, for this beautiful picture is her pride and joy.

The Incomparable Blue Tones of Yves Saint-Laurent's Garden

At Château Gabriel one finds the charm typical of the turn-of-the-century properties in Deauville, moreover the woodwork is

painted in "Deauville green." It is built on the heights and overlooks the town and garden. A lavender-blue stream flows down from the château. It meanders along the green slopes and descends towards the sea—in the meantime irrigating a pool of wonderful blue irises and the fragrant, beautifully planted Jardin Clos.

When the celebrated couturier Yves Saint-Laurent and the prominent businessman Pierre Bergé bought the property, it was a neglected piece of land which had to be completely cleared and cleaned up. They had always been very fond of gardens and in order to reinvent this one they called in specialists. Franz Baechler, the landscape gardener of Swiss origin, listened to their desires and instead of one main garden, created several different smaller ones.

Louis Benech was also involved; he composed a mixed border which extends from the château to the outbuildings. In the Jardin Clos, he planted an herb garden.

The Henri Mestralet company was responsible for the earthworks and the decorator Jacques Grange enhanced the natural surroundings with Napoleon III-style ornaments bought after lively haggling with antique dealers.

The château is approached via a drive planted with evergreen shrubs to dress up the winter season: rhododendrons, hollies, laurustinus (*Viburnum tinus*), and camellias.

Sculpted box in all shapes majestically structures the courtyard. It takes the form of a surrounding bank, domes in the flowerbeds, globes on trunks or on the ground, pyramids, and squares. They combine with quantities of Japanese rosebushes and carpets of acanthus, which are remarkable for their deeply cut leaves and spires of elegant flowers.

The rose garden is situated on a raised terrace near the château and can be seen from the drawing room windows. Its outline is simple and geometric. Box squares serve as the setting for the bushes and standards.

Below, a coiling trail of lavender leads to the Japanese garden and a pool bordered by astilbes, primulas, and very beautiful irises. In the month of May, *Iris kaempferi* and common garden irises offer the incomparable blue tones which only this plant can produce: lavender, sky blue, parma violet, azure, cadet, and midnight blue.

The Jardin Clos is on a higher level and is enclosed by walls. One enters through a wooden door and the garden is immediately revealed in all its rich plenitude. The underlying spirit is medieval. A pergola links the two pavilions and is reminiscent of cloistral architecture. The plants correspond to those found in most traditional herb gardens: aromatic lavender, thyme, and santolina; herbs for seasoning such as savory and chives; for medicinal purposes such as sage or achillea; and industrial herbs like the woad *Isatis tinctoria*, which was cultivated in the past to obtain a blue dye similar to indigo. To maintain the equilibrium, a small bank of lavender faces the pergola. Between them the layout is regular, with two paths forming a cross and delimiting squares in the style of most herb gardens. Rows of fruit trees add to the overall geometric effect. They contrast with the remarkably colorful and fragrant plantings. To harmonize with the clematis and the 'Albertine', 'Dorothy Perkins', 'Leverkusen', and 'Weichenblau' roses which smother the pergola, the plants in this secret garden are in pink, blue, white, gray, and yellow tones. Pink like the knotweed *Polygonum campanulatum* and chives, or blue like *Delphinium belladonna*, perovskia, blue cupidone (*Catananche caerulea*), and *Aster frikartii*. White like the *Centranthus ruba* 'Alba', gray like the *Convolvulus cneoum* or the 'Powis Castle' artemisia. Finally, lady's mantle (*Alchemilla mollis*) and verbascum represent the yellow tones.

The Jardin Clos is remarkable for the beauty of its foliage. Most noteworthy are the matte bluish leaves of a rue (*Ruta graveolens*), the glossy chard, not to mention the lacy foliage of a Roman wormwood (*Artemisia pontica*). Santolina, geranium, and artemisia leave a strong smell on one's fingers while flowers like common or cat's valerian (*Valeriana officinalis*) diffuse a deliciously sweet perfume.

This garden is the result of interesting research into plant properties and their decorative value. For the most part, the plants required dry soil and therefore a great deal of sand had to be brought to drain it. The garden is sunny and well-protected. The plants are at their best from June to September for the greater pleasure of the owners, who spend a part of the summer at Château Gabriel.

At Château Gabriel, where Yves Saint-Laurent spends the summer, the courtyard is decorated with a bench and wooden orangery boxes all painted in "Deauville green." It is surrounded by clipped box globes, cones, and standards; azaleas also form evergreen domes. These azaleas are in fact the extremely rare Rhododendron lateritum, imported directly from Japan. Bear's breeches (acanthus), with their geometric flowers and foliage, and rugosa roses (whose flowers give way to fruit), dodge in and out of the clipped vegetation (facing page).

All the windows of the Château Gabriel open onto the gardens. Pyrus salicifolia 'Pendula', a weeping pear tree with willow-like leaves, forms a link with the grayish blue-green woodwork of the house (center).

Embroidery parterres (here at the Château de Sassy) are characteristic of gardens à la française. They are generally of boxwood. In his publication La Théorie et la Pratique de Jardinage, Dezallier d'Argenville (1680-1765) gives advice on how to succeed with this type of planting: "The dwarf boxwood, which is used for parterre embroidery, has to be very young, dense, not too dry, and the leaves small and very delicate . . . if the plants are chosen according to these criteria, it is no longer necessary to replace the parterre every five or six years" (following pages).

73

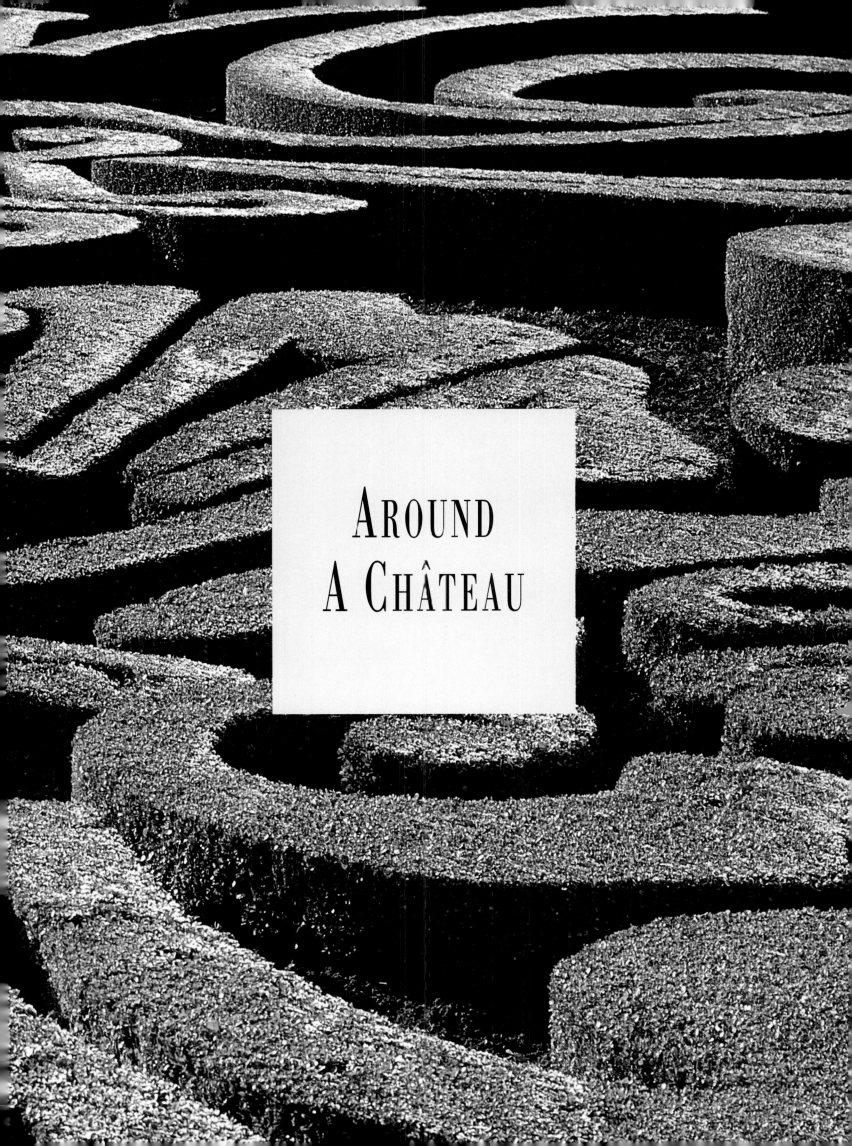

Around
A Château

Château gardens in Normandy followed the general evolution in the art of French gardens, adapting themselves to the changing fashions. After the classic period of formal, rectilinear gardens *à la française*, they converted to the romantic fantasy embodied in the studiously free-form English style.

Today Normandy is restoring its parks and gardens. The province sets a great deal of store by its architectural and plant heritage. The Chartreuses walled gardens at the Château de Canon are filled with flowers; the water scenes have come to life again at Bizy; and Bailleul is the richer for a maze. The past is taking on a new life. It is being faithfully restored—and occasionally enhanced with a contemporary touch.

Sometimes, however, less benign modern influences encroach upon these green worlds and they have to fight to preserve their beauty. This is unfortunately the case at Orcher. This park and château are perched on the edge of a cliff overlooking the Seine. Formerly the site was isolated and romantic, the château with its copses and palisade dominated the marshes that resulted from the diversion of the Seine. In 1930, however, industrialization invaded the estuary and today the gardens and terraces look down over a tormented, grating universe of a sinister and menacing aspect. A noisy world of metal and iron, in which civilization is progressing to the detriment of the landscape. But the garden will not give way. A plant fair takes place there every autumn which assembles nature lovers who are full of hope for the future.

The Orne department, in contrast, provides a peaceful setting for its Mansart-style châteaux. Villers, situated between L'Aigle and Vimoutiers, was built during the sixteenth and seventeenth centuries. Its park dates from the eighteenth century and is laid out in the English style. It features decorative garden constructions like a four-columned temple of neoclassic design called Le Trianon, which serves as a summerhouse. Behind it a large circular hollow has been dug in the earth. It is known as the "Rond des Bonnes Gens," (The Good People's Circle), where the workers used to dance at harvest time. Formerly, the small hill called Snail Mountain sheltered a *glacière* (outdoor icehouse), whose source

was a small waterway called the Stringbean Canal. The grounds are planted with beech, oak, and chestnut, and a majestic approachway, The Grand Avenue, bordered by a double row of chestnut trees and a double bridle path, forms the link between the château and the Norman countryside.

The architecture of the château at the Haras du Pin, not far from Villers, is also attributed to Jules Hardouin-Mansart. It was Louis XIV's finance minister, Jean-Baptiste Colbert, who commissioned this stud farm, which is certainly the most spectacular in the region. The gardens are attributed to André Le Nôtre, who directed the plantings at Versailles. From one side, three straight avenues fan out, crossing the tall clusters of trees which face the stables and the outbuildings arrayed in the form of a horseshoe. On the opposite side and facing south, the terraced gardens rise in tiers from the elevated ground on which the château imposingly stands. The tiers contain the *broderie*, or "embroidery," boxwood themes favored by Le Nôtre, who gradually let nature express itself in the distant perspective over the Norman farmlands.

In general, sculpted vegetation is well-suited to the imposing style of most château architecture. The controlled geometric designs of the greenery and the masonry create a well-balanced harmony. The Beaumesnil château in the Eure department is counterbalanced by an astonishing maze planted in the moats, quite near this baroque castle, which creates a surprising and magnificent effect. Meanwhile, a green dome of yew and boxwood holds sway in the main courtyard.

In a similar vein, at the Champ de La Pierre garden in the Orne department, the eighteenth-century château grounds contain two hornbeam mazes near a beautiful ornamental lake. One's pattern consists of truncated lines; the other's of coils circling around a statue.

The water theme is also very evident at château grounds in Normandy. One example is the Château d'O, which is a perfect gem. It is situated in the Orne department near Mortrée and harmoniously combines Gothic, Renaissance, and Henri IV styles. Its elegant, refined outline is reflected in the moat's waters, which are sometimes sluiced by architectural

*The park at
the Château de Bailleul,
near Fécamp, was
replanted in the
nineteenth century.
It is remarkable for
its avenues of majestic
beeches. Near the
château the walks are
adorned with mossy
statues (facing page).*

elements adorned with balustrades, and sometimes free-flowing and of a wilder nature. In 1985, the proprietor of the Château d'O, Madame de Lacretelle, requested the landscaper Alain Richert to redesign the garden. The latter likes to live on the site where he works. When he moved into the Château d'O, he found only lawns and walls. No trace of the old gardens remained either on the grounds or in the archives. He designed a terraced garden associating fruit trees and rose-

bushes. The first terrace is bordered by a row of ornamental apple trees; the second by apple trees trained on low cords and interspersed with gooseberry bushes; the third by apple trees trained in crisscross fashion; and the fourth by the back wall, against which are trellised espaliered pear trees.

Vendeuvre, near Saint-Pierre-sur-Dives in the Calvados department, is also a water garden. The grounds are in constant evolution; the comte and the comtesse of Vendeuvre are restoring the ornamental lakes and decorative garden constructions and intend to devote Vendeuvre to dancing waters. Cascades, streams, a serpentine, a water staircase, a water tree, a *buffet d'eau*, and fountains animate the walk, which leads from one island to the next.

The Maze at the Château de Bailleul

The elegant and mysterious Château de Bailleul in the Caux region is built in the Renaissance style. It is white and silver and situated in the center of a park planted with beeches of a rare and majestic beauty. The interior decorator Kim Moltzer is very attached to this property, which belongs to his wife's family, and he has embellished the grounds by creating thematic gardens.

Recently he designed a maze, which, although only planted in 1988, already is in impressive shape. This is due to the fast-growing hornbeams which compose it, as well as to the sheer number of trees Kim Moltzer planted: forty-two hundred, clipped in square shapes. The maze is fifty meters long, and the total circuit covers nearly a kilometer. In other words, if one does not follow the correct itinerary or retrace one's steps, one could walk for more than half a mile. Normally it is quite easy to find one's way out as the layout is not complicated. But if it is not a frightening maze, it is fascinating all the same.

Like all garden mazes, it is supposed to symbolize the complexities of existence. Here at Bailleul, it follows the gentle slope of what was formerly a pasture and spreads out at the foot of a dovecote, from which one can study

*The herb garden
situated near the chapel
is composed of geometric
beds. Enormous clumps
of Gunnera manicata
separate it from the
maze, which coils
around the dovecote
(following pages).*

its geometry. It coils around the dovecote and succeeds in unifying this rustic, typically Norman edifice with the formal grounds. Kim Moltzer intends to install a belvedere, or lookout point, in the herb garden he has planted opposite the maze. The latter's clipped architecture will then be visible from this second vantage point.

This maze is one of the largest in France. It requires three days' pruning four or five times a year, depending on the growth of the hornbeams. In winter it is dormant. The leaves turn dry but do not fall, rendering the green walls everpresent and beautiful all the year round.

The Elegance of the Hornbeams at the Château de Limpiville

Also in the Caux region and not far from Bailleul stands the Château de Limpiville, which is renowned for its hornbeams. They are reminiscent of those of Beloeil in Belgium, the work of the prince de Ligne. Beloeil and Limpiville also share a certain rigor, beautiful greenery, and graceful elegance with its hint of fantasy.

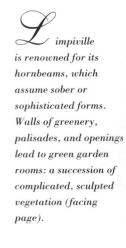

Both the grounds and the Louis XIII château, with its pink-toned bricks and slate roofs, were modified in 1736 by one Dyel de Vaudrocque, who added to the main building two wings surrounded by gardens, which he laid out according to the reigning fashion.

The marquis and marquise of Lilliers took possession of the property in the 1950s. The restoration works were skillfully carried out according to the original, unsigned plans. The former layout was retained and the hedges were clipped and rejuvenated, which contributed to the refurbishment of the grounds.

In order to get one's bearings in the gardens, it helps to know that the main courtyard faces east. In front of the château an immense perspective opens out and then gradually narrows, creating the illusion of parallel lines in the direction of the farm. In the distance one can discern an apple orchard with its rows of fruit trees guarded by a large dovecote.

Then one strays into a small, gently sloping valley which leads to a flat garden of a symmetrical design similar to that in the main courtyard, but on a lower level. An ornamental lake, a *tapis vert*, and rows of hornbeams create a harmonious, rational, reassuring, and perfect layout. A beautiful staircase is set off by

The French-style gardens of the Château de Limpiville, in the Caux region, set the scene for hornbeam walls, statues, and water mirrors in which the gardens are reflected (center).
In keeping with the conception of gardens à la française, the vegetation is architectural, and composed of geometric hedges and clipped yew cones symmetrically disposed in relation to an axis (below).

Limpiville is renowned for its hornbeams, which assume sober or sophisticated forms. Walls of greenery, palisades, and openings lead to green garden rooms: a succession of complicated, sculpted vegetation (facing page).

an amusing fantasy: hornbeams planted in horse-shoe forms interlaced with flat-clipped elms.

One proceeds under the hornbeams, a genuine masterpiece of plant architecture, where long green corridors are enhanced by arcades in the form of double lyres. The entwined lyres are judiciously oriented, one facing the rising and the other facing the setting sun. The shady walk continues between walls of greenery, through cool garden rooms and under domes, arcades, archways, and canopies of alternating hornbeams and beeches.

Finally one comes across a green compartment containing a rose garden, a bowling green, and an amphitheater lawn. The circuit is completed by an esplanade where an obelisk stands tall. On the way back towards the

front of and behind the château, a green carpet spreads out like a great breath of fresh air. One side is framed by a double row of lindens, the other by conifers planted at regular intervals. Here one finds the French-style garden which was restored and replanted in 1925.

The visitor can admire the garden on two levels: one horizontal, the other vertical. The horizontal view offers hornbeam walks which trace perspectives and crossroads and lead to two green compartments, the Leisure Garden and the Games Garden. Vertically, one can distinguish several levels of vegetation: clipped hornbeams; free-growing rhododendrons; disciplined rows of lindens; and a beech hedge which is pink in spring, purple in summer, and flame-colored in autumn.

Behind the Château de Launay stretches a green carpet punctuated with fastigiate yews, and a weeping beech spreads its long sinuous branches. Here and there hornbeam hedges trace green garden rooms.

The Château de Limpiville is reached by a long avenue that creates a link between the landscape of the Caux region and the French-style gardens. The beeches are aligned but their boughs enjoy total liberty (facing page).

château one comes across a part of the park which has recently been restored by Samuel Craquelin, a young Norman landscaper.

The Weeping Beech at the Château de Launay

The eighteenth-century Château de Launay is found across the Seine, not far from the Bec-Hellouin Abbey, just south of Pont-Audemer.

On arrival, one is immediately drawn by the sixteenth-century outbuildings and the half-timbered, tiled dovecote in stone and flint. The château is built in a sober, elegant style which sets the tone for splendid gardens of a pure and well-proportioned design. Both in

The garden is dominated by a weeping beech of exceptional size, which belies the slenderness of its perpetually swaying branches.

Opposite this green garden is a typically Norman kitchen garden. Divided into six squares on either side of a central path, it combines flowers, fruit, and vegetables—all in the most exuberant of hues. One finds nasturtiums, marigolds, dahlias, gladioli, zinnias, African (also called Aztec) marigolds, cosmos, and above all a variety of good things to eat such as pears, raspberries, gooseberries, black currants, and rhubarb.

Beyond the kitchen garden, the farm buildings take one way back into the past. The sheepfold, stable, barn, and cider press probably all date from the sixteenth century and appear to be perfectly intact. At the Château

de Launay the gardens were conceived in the same vein as the buildings, full of contrasts as regards style, mood, and color, and they show each other off to perfection.

Jean de La Varende's Topiaries at Bonneville

Let us now go to the Ouche region and discover Bonneville and its topiaries. Bonneville is the domain that belonged to Jean de La Varende, the writer who made a name for himself in 1934 with a series of Norman stories entitled *Pays d'Ouche.* "Peace, indolence, torpor, dream," are how he described these plains, which served as a setting for his tales. Before becoming a writer he was an artist, which explains his talents as plantsman.

At that time, the un-imposing brick and stone Louis XIII château was set in gardens designed in the English style. La Var-ende added a garden *à la française* punctuated by clipped shrubs. He amused himself by creating a topi-ary chess game. The king, queen, and bishop, the castles, the row of pawns at the back—all in clipped yew—are still there today. Their very elaborate forms are carefully trimmed with

shears every summer, which takes between two weeks and one month, depending on the difficulties encountered and the availability of the gardener.

These topiary forms are symmetrical and are disposed in relation to an axis which opens a perspective onto the Norman countryside. Scots pines serve as a backdrop. The strict contours of the topiaries contrast prettily with those of the disheveled pines. Jean de La Varende also created an Italianate garden, complete with statues, as he was particularly fond of the Florentine style.

He loved this countryside with its incredible greenness and on the grounds of his château he planted a great quantity of vegetation to illus-trate all the nuances of that particular color.

Today Madame de La Varende is restoring the park and also the old orchard by which she sets great store—and is prepar-ing Bonneville for its next century.

The Ornamental Architecture and the Chartreuses Gardens at Canon

At Canon, in the Calvados department, a long avenue bordered by lindens and chestnuts leads to the pale, rectangular, classic

château whose roof is adorned with an Italianate balustrade. The garden scenes, under the arcades formed by the trees, are of great beauty.

The grounds at Canon reflect several styles. First the eighteenth-century French style, with the château set in the center of a geometric layout. Then the pre-Romantic English style—just after the French Revolution, the former proprietor and creator of these gardens, Elie de Beaumont, drew inspiration for the overall layout from the grounds at Stowe in Buckinghamshire and from Kew Gardens. Beaumont, a lawyer and friend of Voltaire, had spent time in England and he loved the irregular designs of the gardens then in fashion there, which idealized nature without ever constraining it. He also let himself be influenced by the ideas of Jean-Jacques Rousseau and by the paintings of Claude Lorrain, Hubert Robert, and Nicolas Poussin. He was very enthusiastic about these idyllic illustrations of nature complete with ruins, kiosks, pagodas, or temples; these surprising and whimsical places made for meditation and philosophizing, to which Canon lent itself equally well.

When strolling in the grounds one comes across these ornamental constructions, set in hornbeam copses surrounded

by an evergreen decor. The central axis parallel to the château sets off to the Temple de la Pleureuse (Temple of the Weeping Woman) on the left, which Elie de Beaumont dedicated to his deceased wife. To the right, it leads to the Chinese Kiosk, which was purchased at the Château des Ternes in Paris and reconstructed at Canon after the death of the park's creator. The dovecote and the vestiges of the Château Béranger with its Renaissance towers shelter in copses along winding avenues, not far from the *miroir d'eau*, or reflecting pool, in which the château is mirrored.

Just beyond the outbuildings and the White Farm stretches a series of gardens known as Les Chartreuses, a pure masterpiece which we also owe to Elie de Beaumont. He wanted to plant orchards and to this end he built thirteen walled gardens linked by six openings. He named the gardens in commemoration of the Carthusian monastery in Paris, near the Jardin du Luxembourg, which supplied him with most of his fruit trees. In these orchards grapes, peaches, pears, apples, almonds, and figs once ripened at leisure, protected and warmed by the walls.

Today the orchards are also flower gardens. Each compartment possesses its own color theme. Masses of pink and red dahlias,

The park at Bizy, near Vernon, is renowned for its magnificent water cascade (now under restoration) seen here from the door of the stables (below). There are also numerous fountains (here the one situated in the Venus Wood) which evoke the baroque splendor of the seventeenth century (above).

marigolds, phlox, cosmos, solidago (commonly known as goldenrod), tickseed (coreopsis), and sneezeweed (helenium) enhance what was formerly a gourmet temple. The continuity and the perspective; the arches; the distant statue of Pomona, goddess of fruit trees; the profusion of tender flowers on old mossy stones; the walls enclosing each intimate garden; and the play of light and shadow transform this place into an infinitely romantic picture. Today it is the Mézerac family that watches over its beauty.

The Splendor of the Fountains at Bizy

Whether it be gushing, streaming, jetting, or still, water occupies the place of honor at Bizy. Situated near the Seine in the vicinity of the town of Vernon, Bizy is a château which was rebuilt during the Second Empire. The façades are inspired by those of a Roman palace and the décor is Louis XVI. Bizy is also a park whose history is somewhat uncertain, although three main periods can be distinguished.

It is said to have first belonged to a certain Nicolas Joubert de Bouville.

The memoirist Louis de Saint-Simon relates that the former possessed "a small place called Bizy, well-situated, which he decorated in a style befitting the bourgeois he was, and which Belle-Isle, after he acquired it, has made into a residence eminently worthy of a son of France." In about 1720, Bizy came into the hands of this duc de Belle-Isle, who commissioned Le Nôtre's son-in-law, Desgot, to design the layout for the grounds. He created a classic park *à la française*, with axes, star-shaped crossroads, and embroidered parterres. The latter were eliminated, but the axes remain, such as the Avenue des Capucins. Bordered with lindens, it links the château to the town of Vernon. In a clearing, at one of the crossroads, one comes across a large circle of earth called Le Manège (the Riding School) where the horses were trained. Farther away, on a hillside, a bowling green forms a vast platform which is attained by two monumental ramps.

Twenty years later, the duc de Belle-Isle, by then a field marshal, commissioned the architect Contant d'Ivry to redesign the park. In this case it is certain that we owe to him the water scenes centered around the château. The water flowed down the steps through a corridor of greenery bordered by clipped yew walls into the Sea Horse Pond and then

The gardens were first laid out in accordance with a classic, early eighteenth-century design. King Louis-Philippe later transformed them into the English style, punctuated with clumps of trees which today are very majestic (facing page).

At Bizy, one comes across beautiful ornamental ponds when walking around the grounds. Here, the one in the Venus Wood.

The French-style garden at Sassy, in the Orne department, is situated below the château. One has to descend several terraces linked by central staircases in order to reach it. However, it is from above that it is most beautiful (facing page).

At Sassy, the well-balanced, symmetrical, and elaborate embroidery parterres were created at the beginning of the twentieth century in the former kitchen garden, whose ornamental pond remains the center of the composition. Frost creates a white veil which accentuates the geometric design (following pages).

Brécy is a well-proportioned, rhythmical masterpiece. One senses the Italian influence, upon which the previous owner, the academician Jacques de Lacretelle, reflects: "As in the Italian comedies, Brécy wears a mask . . . Who was that fanciful organizer, that singular master of ceremonies, most certainly bewitched by the perspectives of Rome or Brenta, who decided to transplant to Normandy an art so foreign to our gardens?"

disappeared. It flowed secretly under the sumptuous stables to supply the area where the horses were washed, which is served by two majestic, symmetrical ramps. Once more the water became invisible, coursed under the château, and reappeared in the park to spurt up in the center of an ornamental lake of harmonious baroque contours, surrounded by colonnades.

It was in this garden that the field marshal Belle-Isle gave a sumptuous reception in honor of Louis XV and Madame de Pompadour.

At the end of the eighteenth century, Bizy became one of the residences of the duc de Penthièvre. After many vicissitudes, the Bizy domain was taken over by King Louis-Philippe, who had the park redesigned in the English style. The trees which stand today were planted during that period. In 1858, the baron de Schickler took up residence at Bizy. His descendants are currently applying themselves to restoring the grounds and making the waters dance again thanks to a gravitation system fed by spring water. These springs have their source higher up in the hills in the village of Bizy and subsequently flow into the Seine, which meanders in the valley below.

Boxwood Embroidery at the Château de Sassy

The Château de Sassy is situated farther south in the Orne department, in the heart of the Argentan plain farmlands. First one strolls through the undulating park planted with myriads of flowers which thrive in the mild Normandy climate, and cascades of lilac growing in the shade of cedars, beeches, and chestnuts. Then, after crossing the main courtyard and skirting the seventeenth-century château of rose-colored brick and white stone, dear to Jean de La Varende, one reaches a spectacular garden *à la française*, which is a model of its kind.

It is quite astonishing, just as though an embroidered carpet had been rolled out far below the château, at the foot of three terraces linked by central staircases with symmetrical flights of steps.

The equilibrium, the proportions, and the composition are perfect. It is enclosed by yew hedges, except on the side parallel to the château, which is linked by water-filled moats. The castle is bordered by an avenue punctuated by perfectly pruned boxwood balls and cubes, and yews clipped into truncated cones. The central axis focuses on a pavilion which faces the château. It is flanked by two monumental fastigiate yews. Here and there the structure is prolonged by two double rows of marquise-shaped clipped lindens. Also in the center, a curved ornamental lake is framed in a *broderie* parterre setting. To the right and left, in perfect symmetry and running the full length of the garden, are two large swaths of *broderie* composed in the same manner, in boxwood arabesques with crushed brick filling the hollows. These sophisticated motifs are on a slightly lower level than the peripheral avenue.

To do this garden justice, one should contemplate it from the uppermost terrace. From

there one can admire its amplitude and appreciate all the details. The strictness of the design provides a striking contrast to the soft contours of the pastures, which are graced with clumps of fruit trees and thoroughbred horses. All is peaceful. One can hear birdsong and the distant neighing and snorting of the bloodstock. There is a magnificent view over the undulating countryside in which hedges trace ribbons somewhat reminiscent of the Haras du Pin. It is indeed the same landscape, the same Normandy.

The garden at the Château de Sassy was created in 1910, taking the place of the former walled kitchen garden—with its regular design of symmetrical squares bordered by rows of fruit trees and in the center, the famous circular pool. Greenhouses with arched glass roofs lined the far wall.

The duc d'Audiffret-Pasquier is the present proprietor of the Château de Sassy. His father commissioned Achille Duchêne, who drew inspiration from a drawing by Le Nôtre, to create this French-style garden. One recognizes the mastery of a great artist who designed the grounds in harmony with the château and yet integrated it perfectly into the Norman landscape. This garden is unchanging and indifferent to the passage of time. Snow enhances it, frost transfigures the architecture and motifs, and magic takes over.

The Terraced Garden at the Château de Brécy

Most châteaux are built on an elevated site and dominate the grounds. The opposite is true at Brécy. Here the terraced gardens, which extend from the sober, symmetrical, seventeenth-century château, are laid out on the slopes of a hill between the plains of Bayeux and Caen, and rise in tiers towards heavily worked metal gates which open onto the sky.

These embroidery-style gardens, traditionally attributed to François Mansart, are also thought to date from the seventeenth century. Today, Monsieur and Madame Didier Wirth are applying themselves to restoring and bringing them new life.

The visit commences with a modern fantasy, a pocket herb garden, which is nonetheless in the spirit of classic gardens. It is of a square design and structured by checkerboard boxwood, which portions out spaces for thyme, rosemary, mint, tarragon, savory, and, in the center, for a flowerpot containing a standard laurel.

After the herb garden, one can admire the spectacle of the terraced gardens rising in five tiers, which are buttressed by support walls graced with stone ornaments. The latter are omnipresent at Brécy, embellishing the gardens and adding to their attraction. Pilasters surmounted by vases, ingenious staircases, consoles, and balusters are reminiscent of the most sophisticated Italian gardens. However, the box embroidery motifs in the lower terraces—inspired by the illustrated eighteenth-century work *Le Jardin de Plaisir* (by the celebrated architect and garden designer André Mollet)—follow the pure tradition of French-style gardens. Central staircases lead to the second level where paths divide up triangular parterres and converge towards crossroads planted with box cones. Torsade (helix)-shaped box topiaries and clipped cone-shaped yews border the terraces.

Lions flank the steps which lead to the third level. There, a large green lawn sets off two basins of classical arabesque design. Various perennials brighten the fourth terrace's support wall.

The central staircase is surmounted by vases. At the top a narrower walk leads to the secret gardens: a rose garden on the right, and a kitchen garden on the left planted with salad vegetables, chives, cabbages, and sorrel, accompanied by marigolds and Jacob's ladder (polemonium).

A staircase leads to the fifth terrace, which is bordered by balustrades, these again surmounted by vases. It is also enhanced by two pavilions over which climb a pair of white clematis *C. wilsonii*. The axis, aligned with the central window of the château, culminates on the fifth terrace with very elaborate gates of great beauty, probably forged by Isaac Geslin.

The gardens at Brécy are well-balanced and beautifully rational. The stonework and the vegetation are in unison, both being of elaborate and sophisticated conception. Perfect harmony exists between the atmosphere of the village, seemingly untouched by progress, and the gardens with their unshakable serenity.

The gardens at Brécy were designed to be seen from the château, where one can enjoy a view over the five terraces. Here the wall which separates the first terrace from the second is punctuated with vases and adorned with honeysuckle and boxwood, which transform it into a rampart of vegetation.

The two last flights of steps which separate the terraces are flanked by pillars surmounted by vases, which create a spectacular contrast between the stone and the elegant delicacy of the wrought iron design (facing page).

These 'Pink Pearl' rhododendrons, with white 'Purity' in the background, were planted about eighty years ago by Guillaume Mallet at the Bois des Moutiers in Varengeville-sur-Mer. They are situated close to the house in the level part of the garden. They have since been nurtured and pruned, which is why they are so dense and prolific. The soil and the climate of Varengeville suit them perfectly (following pages).

ENGLISH STYLE

ENGLISH
STYLE

The English influence is strongly evident in Normandy and is no doubt
due to the proximity and the similari-
ty of the two climates. The south
coast of Great Britain is of course even milder
than the Normandy coast, but the landscapes
have many elements in common. Maupassant
goes even further: he was enchanted by "the
melancholy aspect of the great rolling Norman
countryside, resembling an immense English
garden of vast inordinate proportions where
the farmyards, surrounded by two or four
rows of trees and full of short, bushy apple
trees masking the buildings, trace prospects of
woods, copses, and shrubberies as far as the
eye can see."

Practically the same range of plants can be
cultivated in both coun-
tries. Many Norman land-
scapers are inspired by
English gardens, likewise
their British counterparts
often look to France. Illustrating this point are the
experiences of the following Norman landscape
gardeners. The comtesse
de Vogüé, creator of the
celebrated Miromesnil
potager (see p. 152), never
missed her annual trips to
London at the end of May
to see the latest achieve-
ments on exhibit at the
Chelsea Flower Show.
Doctor Evrard (see p.
185), a collector of peren-
nial geraniums, maintains close contact with
Mr. and Mrs. Norton (who are themselves specialists on the subject and have taken over the
East Lambrook garden in Somerset, originally
created by Margery Fish). Martine Lemonnier's fascination (see p. 181) for the
meconopsis (blue poppy) stems from a visit to
the Edinburgh botanical gardens. When
creating and planting her flowerbeds at Vasterival, Princesse Sturdza (see p. 177) drew
inspiration from Knightshayes in Devon.

Furthermore, Robert de Bosmelet, who is
currently restoring the gardens of the Château
de Bosmelet, encourages exchanges and com-
parisons between Normandy and the counties
in the south of England. His mother was English and fascinated by gardens, and it is to her
that he owes his introduction to certain rare
plants found there. She made Bosmelet into a
"Franglais" garden. Her son studied at Oxford
and in his capacity as the president of the
Association France–Grande-Bretagne, he
hopes to make the gardens on either side of the
Channel both known and loved.

Norman garden initiatives are not exclusively claimed by natives; noteworthy creations
also can be attributed to English landscape
gardeners, whose identities are not always
known. This is the case at Nacqueville, where
it is known from reliable sources that Hippolyte de Tocqueville followed the advice of an
English landscaper, but no further details are
available. On the other hand, it is certain that
Miss Lloyd Jones worked at Pontrancart at the
beginning of the century. It was she who
orchestrated the colors of the borders in the
flower labyrinth. Lanning Roper, an American, who in the sixties and seventies created
many gardens in England after having taken
up permanent residence there, is said to have
worked near Canon in the Calvados region. It
was of course Gertrude
Jekyll and Edwin Lutyens
who were behind the Bois
des Moutiers masterpiece.
Russell Page designed or
improved many gardens in
Normandy, the most cele-
brated being Varaville,
and more recently Arabella
Lennox-Boyd and Mark
Brown have also designed
gardens there.

Do these creators need
an introduction? Unfortu-
nately very little is known
about Miss Lloyd Jones
who, to all intents and purposes, was very proficient
in blending plants and
color harmonies. She be-
longed to the generation of English gardeners
who lived at the turn of the century.

Miss Jekyll met the architect Edwin
Lutyens in 1889. She was forty-five and he was
twenty. Together they created about a hundred gardens between 1890 and 1914, but not
many of them have survived. They were commissioned by property owners enamored of art
and culture and who favored elegant living.

The gardens designed by Edwin Lutyens
consist of compartments which prolong the
architectural design of the house. Gradually
this domination of man over nature becomes
less marked and in the distance the garden
blends in freely with the landscape. These
coherent designs withstand the test of time,
unlike the intentionally fleeting compositions
created by Miss Jekyll, who possessed a perfect
understanding of plants and a talent for color
harmony. She was in fact an artist and she
composed her flowerbeds as she did her paintings. Her designs for mixed borders show that
she used perennials in elongated clumps so
that the specimens in bloom masked those that

*The
Shakespeare Garden
created by Mark Brown
stretches as far as a
pergola. It contains
plants evoked by the
playwright in his
dramas or poems:
thyme, chives, sage,
columbine, wormwood
(artemisia), savory,
fumitory, catmint
(nepeta), wild pansies,
daisies, irises,
wallflowers, and chervil
(facing page).*

*Madame
Mary Mallet gives all
her care and attention
to the plants at Le Bois
des Moutiers, and
particularly in the
summer to the 'Iceberg'
roses which adorn the
gardens behind the
manor house. In the
spring these same beds
are planted with lily-
flowered 'White
Triumphator' tulips.*

had faded. She was also proficient in the art of staggering the flowerings. She favored theme gardens and in each of the compartments designed by Lutyens, she planned spectacular but ephemeral unfurlings. She created a bulb garden for the spring, an aster garden for September, and a rose garden to give pleasure for the course of the summer. The compartments designed by Lutyens at Moutiers still exist and the plantings remain faithful to Miss Jekyll's style.

Russell Page was born at the beginning of the century. After having studied the fine arts, he became a "gardener" as he liked to call himself. In 1928 he became associated with the landscaper Geoffrey Jellicoe and together they carried out many grand projects. This marked the beginning of Russell Page's international career. In France he laid out gardens where his style, structural layout, and favorite plants can be recognized.

Lanning Roper was an American officer engaged in the Second World War when he first went to England, and it was there that he settled down. He took courses at the Royal Botanical Gardens at Kew and at the Edinburgh Botanical Gardens, then started to design his own. He was modest, had very good taste, and took the trouble to listen to his clients. He was a perfectionist, loved plants, and was very knowledgeable about how to use them. Until his death in 1983, he designed castle and manor house gardens in England and abroad and also worked for the National Trust.

Two contemporary English creators have worked in Normandy: Arabella Lennox-Boyd and Mark Brown. Arabella is Italian and married to an Englishman. She has an inborn sense of the art of gardens. From Italy she inherited a taste for architecture and in England she adopted the poetry of plants. She has designed numerous gardens in England and abroad, including the garden of her childhood friend, the princesse Paola, at the Palais du Belvédère in Belgium.

Mark Brown is a young English landscape gardener who settled in Normandy where he developed a garden design of great subtlety. He listens attentively to his clients and he tries to convert them to his love of plants and his very elaborate associations. He is fascinated by the beauty of nature, which he uses as though he were composing a canvas. He takes in a multitude of details at a glance and transposes them into the scenes which his imagination creates.

These English creators have greatly enriched the province of Normandy. They offered us their knowledge, their comprehension of nature, and above all their vision. They sharpened our outlook and fanned the flame of our passion. The English influence is perpetuated by these designers and by plant exchanges, and gardeners in Normandy have their sights constantly turned towards England.

Edwin Lutyens and Gertrude Jekyll at Le Bois des Moutiers

Two great English garden designers witnessed the creation of Le Bois des Moutiers. Edwin Lutyens designed the house and garden and

Gertrude Jekyll composed the plantings. This magnificent tour de force is situated at Varengeville-sur-Mer, near Dieppe. The elegance of the house and the splendor of the gardens are very moving and are the result of the talent of their prestigious planners and of the determination of a family who continually restores and embellishes the property in the spirit of its creator, Guillaume Mallet. The vision of a beautiful garden enriches the souls of those who contemplate it. Madame Mary Mallet, Guillaume's daughter-in-law, is entranced each day by so much beauty and wants to share it, rather as if she were invested with a mission. It is the beauty itself which gives her the energy. She wants to safeguard it. This feeling of rapture has never left her since

down as far as the sea. He set about looking for a piece of land on the coast near Dieppe where the soil was acidic. There he would be able to cultivate the species he adored. Varengeville seemed to be the ideal village. He acquired about thirty acres which sloped gently down towards the shore.

A friend of his wife, Mrs. Earl, entertained many brilliant intellectuals in her London salon, and notably followers of the Arts and Crafts movement. She advised Guillaume Mallet to acquire the services of Edwin Lutyens, then a young architect. Mrs. Earl was Lutyens's aunt by marriage. She was a very original and artistic lady who dedicated her book entitled *Pot Pourri* to Madame Guillaume Mallet. This work contained her thoughts on plants and gardens.

The Sundial Garden on the grounds of Le Bois des Moutiers is enclosed by yew architecture. In the foreground is a 'Lykkefund' rosebush.

the day it was revealed to her. "Looking back, this experience seems to represent a lifetime . . . from the first day when as a young bride, I came to Varengeville alone to meet my parents-in-law, that unforgettable day when, on opening the discreet gate at Moutiers, I discovered a scene of such beauty that I thanked God for not having seen it before, for fear that I might have married just to be able to live there!" Today, still demonstrating the same fervor, she claims, "Here, beauty is our religion." Her children have followed her in this venture for the greater pleasure of us all.

Guillaume Mallet came from a wealthy, cultured family of garden lovers, had always heard talk about colors, nature, and plants, and was nostalgic about English gardens, especially those of the Isle of Wight, which stretch

The meeting between Edwin Lutyens and Guillaume Mallet took place in 1898. The commission concerned both the house and garden. The house was considered small for that day and age. Guillaume Mallet was not worldly and lived for his family, his garden, and for music. The resulting garden was divided into structured sections, linked by perspectives and planted with daringly luxuriant vegetation in studied color harmonies. Miss Jekyll never went to Moutiers as she walked with difficulty. She was a prodigious writer and sent the plans by mail. Perfect complicity reigned between the three personalities, which is no doubt why they marked this property with such force.

One enters the White Garden by a discreet door in a wall of yews which serves as the setting. From there, one has a view over the green foliage compartments, separated by walls which, like the house, are in brick, wood, and edgewise tiles. Box parterres structure this part of the garden which extends as far as the music room. They are planted with 'White Triumphator' and with other white tulips in the spring, followed by 'Iceberg' roses in the summer. They are interspersed with helleborus or Christmas roses, white bleeding hearts (*Dicentra spectabilis* 'Alba'), divaricatus asters, which Miss Jekyll specially favored, with foxgloves (*Pulmonaria* 'Sissinghurst White'), *Hydrangea involucrata*, camellias, and *Magnolia stellata* 'Water Lily'. Here and there hosta or plantain lily, and lamium (commonly known as deadnettle), serve as groundcover. *Viburnum davidii*, a *V. plicatum* 'Mariesii', a

(*Malva moschata alba*). There is a beautiful climbing rose on the wall of the house, the most delicate and gracious of all, 'General Schablikine'. It bears loose salmon-pink flowers and was obtained in 1878. The sheltered site is ideal as the rose is sensitive to the cold; it is blended here with a pink *Clematis montana*.

After the enchantment of this beautiful association, one turns around to admire the two mixed borders which face each other. They are punctuated by yew ramparts which act as partitions and serve as a setting for the bushes, shrubs, perennials, and bulbs. These flowerbeds are situated at the foot of walls trained with climbing hydrangeas. The color harmonies are mellow and refined. Among the

T he perspective follows an axis parallel to the house, then a series of walled gardens, and is continued with a pergola, favored by Miss Jekyll. Great quantities of roses climb over it, such as the 'Lykkefund' in the foreground on the left, the Rosa willmottiae—a shrub used as a climber— on the right, and the 'Francis E. Lester' in the background on the right.

Magnolia grandiflora, and the naive white flowers of a *Rhodotypos scandens* grow at the foot of the walls along which a climbing *Hydrangea petiolaris*, a white montana clematis, and a 'Madame Alfred Carrière' climbing rose are trained.

Then one passes in front of the Arts and Crafts-style house, where the surroundings are very elaborate. Brick and stone designs decorate the path leading from the White Garden, further extended by the pergola. Four fastigiate trees lend their pyramidal forms to the corners. Most of them are dark yews replacing the original cypresses, which have disappeared. Many shrubs grow at their feet such as rosemary, daphne, and rhododendrons (*R. williamsianum*) interspersed with hosta, white valerian, and white mallow

taller shrubs one finds rhododendrons, rosebushes, silver eleagnus, deutzia, buddleja, and peonies, and among the shorter ones, santolina and hebe.

Ranking among the perennials are valerian, nepeta or catmint, asters, polemonium (commonly known as Jacob's ladder), eryngium or sea holly, meadow rue (thalictrum) iris, phlox, Japanese anemones, and geraniums. Bulbs are represented by tulips, lilies, and *Allium christophii*.

The visit continues under the pergola, a garden element Miss Jekyll adored.

"For some years now we have 'borrowed' the Italian fashion for pergolas," she writes. "In Italy the main function of the pergola is to provide support for the vines and shade for the paths, whereas it plays a more decorative

I t is in March that one should go to see the magnolias which adorn the orchard at Le Bois des Moutiers, here Magnolia × loebneri *(following pages).*

In the clearing, Chinese rhododendrons (R. augustinii) in various shades of blue blend with bluebells (Scilla campanulata) (facing page).

The walled Sundial Garden is close to the house (above). One of the walls is adorned with a 'Wedding Day' rambler (on the left in the photo). On the other side a 'Ballerina' rose is associated with lavender. A 'Fritz Nobis' rosebush is drowning in its petals (below).

role in our gardens." Miss Jekyll combined all kinds of creepers. "The climbing plants which I prefer for pergolas are vine, jasmine, Virginia creeper, aristolochia, and wisteria. I do not recommend roses as they only flower at the top and so one cannot see the blooms." Nevertheless, on the pergola at Moutiers there are some very graceful roses ('Francis Lester', 'Sparrieshoop', 'Lykkefund', and 'Alister Stella Gray', as well as large- or small-flowered clematis (*C. montana*, *C. viticella rubra*, and 'Madame Lecoultre'). One can also see the wide green leaves of a crimson glory vine (*Vitis coignetiae*) which offers a magnificent show of color in the autumn.

The pergola leads into the Sundial Garden on the right, which is planted with 'Ballerina' roses grown as bushes or standards and underplanted with lavender, santolina, and rosemary. Farther on, one comes to the Magnolia Garden, which is a glorious sight in the spring. Along one of the walls there is a mixed border of hydrangeas (*H. paniculata*), 'Penelope' roses, and the bell-shaped pale pink

In the gardens of Le Bois des Moutiers, the Rhododendron halopeanum attain a height of 30 feet. They stand out against a somber, matte backdrop of Atlas cedars (above). Along the riverbanks, the gigantic structured leaves of Gunnera manicata set off the delicacy of the rhododendron flowerings (below).

flowers of *Polygonum campanulatum*, commonly known as knotwood.

The former kitchen garden has been transformed into a rose garden in which the central walk is punctuated by fastigiate yew trees, and is bordered by trellises with 'Helenae', 'Bobbie James', Albéric Barbier', and 'Rambling Rector' climbing roses.

One returns to the pergola by a path bordered with holly and mahonia, which leads down towards the wild garden. However, just before, on the left, one's attention is caught by a terrace near the house bordered by hydrangeas and on the right by a bank designed by Lutyens backed against a yew hedge and surrounded by rhododendrons. These constitute the last architectural motifs, the final visible intervention of the landscaper, who subsequently lets nature take over.

From there one enters into a wild garden created by Guillaume Mallet, inspired by Gertrude Jekyll's texts on woodland gardens. Clearings alternate with forestal scenes. The vegetation traces green or multicolored curves down the slopes of the valleys which lead to the sea.

In May and June the rhododendrons constitute the park's crowning glory: white or cream, deep or pale pink, dark red, or mauve tinted with purple, they attain immeasurable

heights. One single *Rhododendron halopeanum* in the hollow of a small valley constitutes a veritable pale pink mountain of tender and spectacular beauty. Rosebushes, pieris, hollies, holm oaks, arbutus, gaultheria, maples, beeches, and Scots pines (*Pinus sylvestris*) adorn the slopes and protect cascades of *Cornus canadensis* (commonly known as creeping dogwood), squills, ferns, arum lilies (*Zantedeschia aethiopica*), and *Iris kaempferi*. One climbs back up towards the house on a path bordered by a rich bouquet of mollis azaleas in warm tones of yellow, pink, peach, and melon. The gardens are beautiful all the year round: dewy in the spring, vivacious in summer, flamboyant in the autumn, and calm in winter, when the fleshy foliage of the rhododendrons contrasts with the dull needles of the blue cedars—chosen by Guillaume Mallet to harmonize with the sky and sea.

Le Bois des Moutiers is an enchanted place which should be visited in silence in order to appreciate it to the full. It is a family enterprise. "We all make a point of trying to save this spot, of welcoming visitors and sharing these moments with them—which are our greatest encouragement," explains Claire Mallet-Bouchayer, one of Mme. Mallet's daughters. "It is very exhilarating work

Lightness and splendor of the blooms of the Rhododendron halopeanum. At Moutiers they can be admired for about three weeks, from mid-May to early June (facing page).

which sustains us day after day. The visitors seem happy in the park and this encourages them to create beauty and to save other gardens."

Mark Brown, Contemporary Gardener and Landscape Architect

Not far from Le Bois des Moutiers lives Mark Brown, who is an Englishman, a gardener, and a landscape architect. He possesses a highly refined knowledge of plants and he uses them with great finesse.

He sees plants with the perception of an artist and has visited all the best gardens. He reads the specialized reviews and has traveled

The Shakespeare Garden borders the façade of the house, against which English landscaper Mark Brown created an orange theme using poppies (Papaver atlanticum), euphorbia, fennel, sunflowers, and 'Dropmore Scarlet' honeysuckle (facing page).

all over the world botanizing. In Varengeville, a road leads to the renowned Manoir d'Ango, the garden which he created at the end of the 1980s around a long, low, half-timbered house. Both rustic and sophisticated, it is also very Anglo-Norman, even if other influences are present.

This young garden has now come into its own. Varied scenes fan out from the old farmhouse which, in the past, sheltered men and animals alike. The areas treated by Mark Brown give onto a vast meadow, which leads in turn to a cider-apple orchard.

One enters via an enclosed, shady haven where all kinds of green plants thrive and where the flowers, all chosen from the white range, give the impression of being perfectly incidental. The vegetation has been scrupu-

lously studied and very judiciously placed, for Mark Brown knows how to appreciate with precision the beauty of a certain type of bark, a leaf, or the color of a flower. He wanted to make this place into a sort of Japanese jungle in which he combined all sorts of wild plants which take root and self-sow at will. He rarely intervenes and tolerates invasion up to a certain point. He favors vegetation of gracious bearing and instinctively blends plants which require the same conditions of exposure, light, and humidity. Under the pale green indented leaves of the maples, under the katsuras (*Cercidiphyllum japonicum*) with their round fluttering leaves which, in the autumn, diffuse a smell of burnt caramel, under the elegant branches of cornus or dogwood, or in the shel-

ter of the crimped leaves of Japanese hornbeams (*Carpinus japonica*), he planted all sorts of gramineae with trembling tapering foliage, like *Miscanthus sinensis* 'Gracilimus' or *M. sinensis* 'Silver Feather', or evergreen carex. He interspersed them with perennial plants with large round leaves such as rodgersia or *Petasites japonicus* var. *giganteus*; with hydrangeas like the *H. paniculata* 'Kiushu' (whose creamy white flowers resemble lace); with dwarf or giant bamboos; with the bluegreen leaves of plume poppies (*Macleaya cordata*); with the candelabra primula (*P. japonica*); of course with Jacob's ladder (*Polemonium nipponicum* 'Album'); and with all the bulbs that flower to welcome the spring.

On the other side of the house the atmosphere is different due to the sunny exposure.

Gardening in Mark Brown's beds in September. A mixed border in the blue, violet, pink, fuchsia, and purple range: perennial geraniums and tall asters against a purple cotinus.

Mark Brown made a garden out of this very Norman orchard. He simply cut the grass to create square plots of equal size. In the foreground, the Shakespeare Garden; in the background, a beech hedge characteristic of the Caux region (following pages).

The blue sequence in Mark Brown's garden is composed of Siberian flags (Iris sibirica), comfrey (Symphytum caucasicum), columbines, geraniums, and violets (above).

A Ceanothus impressus is trained against the house. This delicate frost-tender plant thrives because of the southerly exposure. It also benefits from the mild climate, which permits it to survive the winter. Its flowers are a heavenly blue, and the minute, aromatic leaves smell of spicebread (below left). This scene in the Shakespeare Garden associates three-colored sage, blue and white Alpine columbines (Aquilegia alpina), catmint (nepeta), a variety of wormwood (Artemisia absinthium), and mint (below right).

Extremely refined scenes brighten up the faded half-timbering; like the one that was inspired by the sunrise in Newhaven during one of Mark Brown's numerous commutes between France and England. He reproduced exactly the same colors using green and colored plants, transposed the same nuances, the same tones and half tones, the same harmonies; all in shades of gray, gray-blue, apricot, salmon, pale yellow, and bronze.

For the gray, he chose the pretty santolina (*S. neapolitanum*) with its fine, silvery foliage and discreet pale yellow flowers, or again wormwood, like the *Artemisia arborescens* 'Faith Raven', which he trained along the walls. For the gray-blue, he planted common rue (*Ruta graveolens*) with its gray-green foliage. In the apricot tones, he cultivated little round-headed chrysanthemums, which are not to be found anywhere else. For the pale yellow he favored red-hot pokers, sometimes known as torch lilies (*Kniphofia* 'Modesta'), which take on an amber tone reminiscent of apple jelly, or the almost white eschscholzia, or again the

autumn-flowering crocus (*Crocus pulchellus*). For the bronze tones he chose fennel (*Foeniculum vulgare* 'Purpureum') with its bronze leaves and a carex of the same color. He drowned all this in a mist of gramineae dominated by golden oats (*Stipa gigantea*).

Continuing along by the house, the colors turn from black to crimson or bluish red, then to orange, brick, and yellow. One flowerbed is entirely in shades of blue, pink, mauve, violet, purple, and plum, with aconitum (commonly known as wolf's bane or monkshood),

bright asters, meadow saffron (colchicum), coneflowers (*Echinacea purpurea*), a *Cotinus* 'Deep Purple', sage (*Salvia nemorosa*), *Verbena bonariensis*, and purple wood spurge (*Euphorbia amygdaloides* 'Rubra'). Purple plantain (*Plantago major* 'Atropurpurea') and the purplish red flowers of oriental Christmas roses enhance the picture.

The Shakespeare Garden is to be found inside the house where Mark Brown has assembled plants mentioned in Shakespeare's *A Midsummer Night's Dream* and *Hamlet.*

Here is what Ophelia says: "There's rosemary, that's for remembrance . . . and there is pansies, that's for thoughts . . . There's fennel for you, and columbines; There's rue for you. . . . There's a daisy. I would give you some violets . . . "

There, in the spring, one finds marigolds, columbines, wormwood, marjoram, sage, cloves, fennel, chamomile, wild pansies, Madonna lilies (*Lilium candidum*), 'Apothecary's rose', or crown imperial (*Fritillaria imperialis*). Little box hedges divide up the space and create partitions for all these plants. They give the effect of tapestries, or slightly faded carpets. Only marigolds or buttercups play the role of lanterns and illuminate the parterre in all seasons.

Farther on, the orchard adorns itself with wild flowers and the meadow is crisscrossed by paths. Although everything is planned, it is skillfully staged in total liberty and very simply but artistically composed.

Gabrielle van Zuylen's Garden, Created by Russell Page

Russell Page designed many gardens in Normandy, among which figures one at the stud farm of Varaville near Deauville. From the outset one recognizes his style by the strong and well-proportioned architectural greenery. The baron and baronesse van Zuylen asked him to create this décor in 1966. They made his acquaintance during the course of a lunch with neighboring friends soon after having acquired the Varaville stud farm. The site was very poetic with its beautiful eighteenth-century stables. In 1937 the castle had burned and it proved impossible to restore the ruins. They therefore decided to build a new, resolutely modern residence. This task fell to the American architect Peter Harnden.

Russell Page did not approve of the design, but in the face of Gabrielle van Zuylen's insistence, he yielded and put all his talent and genius into planting this garden. His task was by no means easy. How was he to go about linking the classic stables with an avant-garde construction and integrating a structured foliage architecture in the midst of the very pastoral Norman landscape, enhanced, moreover, by grazing horses? He applied the principle which he expresses in his publication, *The Education of a Gardener*: "The problem for a garden-maker is always the same, and I always try to discover in what consists the significance of the site, and then base my garden theme on that. For a theme of some kind, a basic idea is essential." It was therefore decided that the garden would not exceed the limits of the old kitchen garden. It would be protected by walls and inaccessible to the horses. Russell Page divided the space up with yew hedges and designed compartments of greenery. For, to quote him once more, "In a garden, as elsewhere, good design is simple design, whether in its general disposition or in detail. It is better to make a statement emphatically and once only." The compartments are linked by paths and each one can be discovered during the course of a walk in which one goes from one surprise to another. A White Garden is planted with 'Iceberg' roses, which are dominated by geometric clipped yews. The Garden of Squares is composed of thirty-six parterres enclosed by boxwood. Today the garden is green and serene.

The Summer Garden is white, blue, and gray. White like the lupins or delphiniums. Blue like irises or columbine. Gray like santolina, *Stachys lanata*, or the weeping pear tree *Pyrus salicifolia* 'Pendula' whose silvery leaves bend to stroke a bench where tea is taken. These plants are assembled in beds around a lawn and planted in complete liberty in the English style.

Russell Page designed the site to have charm and rigor. It is the illustration of the mastery of an architect, the application of a perfectionist, and the refined taste of an enlightened plant lover. In this he was succeeded by Gabrielle van Zuylen, great connoisseur and garden lover, who has published several works on this art, including one entirely devoted to Russell Page's gardens. According to her whims and passions, Baronesse van Zuylen modified the plantings, but maintained the architectural structure. So while remaining faithful to the original idea, it radiates a charm which is the result of an alchemy between the talent of a great creator and the experience of an enlightened gardener who listens each day to the pulse of her garden.

In the garden of the Varaville stud farm, one recognizes Russell Page's rigorous architecture, materialized with yew hedges. "First in Western Europe, I would place the ordinary yew, Taxus baccata, as an evergreen of many garden uses. You may use it as a feathery bush . . . you may clip it into hedges . . . or give it any shape you like. Lightly clipped over each year, you can use it as a close-textured green backdrop for other plantings." (Russell Page, The Education of a Gardener.)

I try to come to my planting problems as an architect. My first concern is with volumes, textures and with the construction of my plant material: then as a painter, I must deal with colour for its own sake . . . finally as a gardener, I have to decide which plants I can use and in what combinations." Russell Page, The Education of a Gardener (at Varaville, facing page).

The water garden at Giverny and its water lilies fascinated and obsessed Monet. He painted them incessantly: "I have once more started things that are impossible to do: grass swaying at the bottom of the water . . . it is admirable to see, one can go mad by wanting to paint that," he wrote in 1890. This photo could have inspired Reflets verts, the celebrated canvas at the Orangerie des Tuileries museum in Paris (following pages).

WATER
GARDENS

Normandy is a fresh, mild land—a fertile countryside glistening in countless shades of green. Water abounds and enriches the earth and the gardens—water from the sky, the rivers, the ponds, and the sea. It blends the colors and unifies the Norman landscape, which in turn is reflected in it.

The rain gently veils the plants, which revel in it—except when the elements grow angry and storms rage over the Cotentin peninsula. But this is an extremely rare occurrence. For the most part, the farmland hedges are adequate protection against the rain and spray, and maintain a cool enclosure for the plants. The clouds are drawn towards the forests, and the sea softens the temperatures all year round.

Here, even if someone decides to amuse himself with the water—for example, to capture and calm it, retain it, make it dance, accelerate it, or adorn it with plants, discretion nevertheless rules. Ultimately, water has free rein. And if this person ever were to go so far as to create a body of water from start to finish, the natural elements would be respected and the garden would blend into the landscape. Nature would be the model, simulated and idealized, recreating the sinuous, unpredictable contours of the ponds and rivers. An image of an untamed landscape reinvented. We are a long way from the fountains of the Villa d'Este, the sublime but constraining architecture of Versailles's Grand Canal or the crowning piece among its *Grandes Eaux*: the Neptune Fountain.

Garden art has often wavered between two extremes. In the eighteenth century, it freed itself from strictly ordered Cartesian principles and escaped to romanticism. Almost a century later, it broke from the Victorian yoke and mosaic-style cultivation, converting to the English landscaper William Robinson's natural planting method. This art was reconciled with nature more than once.

Norman gardens reflect this evolution. Nacqueville, for example, is a romantic garden which was conceived in accordance with the fashion at that time, that is to say it turned away from the gardens *à la française*. The water gardens at Pontrancart and Plantbessin are recent creations which conform with the contemporary English conception of garden art.

Giverny offers visual proof that a water garden allows the creation of spectacular effects in a limited space. Here generous plants that are not particularly demanding and prolific flowering plants that glisten and create an attractive luxuriance mingle with those which grow in or near the water, in a reinvented setting of willows, poplars, and bald cypresses.

Normandy lends itself to tranquil water gardens. The water that nature provided was a blessing that gardeners could hardly ignore. They created what Marcel Proust called "floating flowerbeds" or "celestial parterres." For water gives "flowers a setting of a more precious and moving color than the color of the flowers themselves." These gardeners offer us their refreshing and musical interpretation of an earthly paradise of exceptional greenery.

The Romantic Gardens of the Château de Nacqueville at the Tip of the Cotentin Peninsula

In a garden, water is the source of fertility and felicity. Nacqueville takes full advantage of this element, for spring-fed water and rain are in constant supply.

Nacqueville is situated at the tip of the Cotentin, a mere stone's throw from the sea. Near enough to benefit from its mildness, but not so close as to be inconvenienced by the spray. Protected from the west winds, the garden is situated in a sheltered position in the hollow of a valley. The Castellets river flows through this vale and the successive designers of this garden were in the habit of toying with it. Nacqueville is a vision in mauve and green. Mauve because of the profusion of rhododendrons which flower in the spring, and green because of the water which abounds.

This romantic park was created in 1830, whereas the château was built three centuries earlier. The garden was the dream of proprietor Hippolyte de Tocqueville, the elder brother of Alexis. The latter wrote in the following terms to a friend in 1857: "Yesterday I visited my brother Hippolyte. They have put enough money and taste into Nacqueville to make it one of the prettiest places in the world." Following several years spent in England, Hippolyte went back to France with a pronounced liking for gardens. He

The grounds of the Château de Nacqueville are planted with rhododendrons and old hybrids whose delicate colors are delightful (above). Near the manor house the owners have planted clumps of azaleas, which they have combined with other heath-mold shrubs (below).

followed the advice of an English landscaper (whose identity is unknown to us) and fixed his objectives at Nacqueville. First he decided to create water scenes: a pond, waterfalls, and fountains, which would enliven the valley. Then he planted a lawn of vast dimensions, like a great breath of fresh air, to serve as a setting for the château. He also decided to divert the approachway so one would come upon the château by surprise. Lastly he decided to surround the park with tall trees to create an impression of mystery.

Then Nacqueville changed hands. "Forty years later," relates the present owner, Monsieur Azan, "my wife's great-grandfather decided to improve the park. He was a remarkable man, a specialist in hydraulics, who had built bridges and dams all over the world." The said man, Hildevert Hersent, who had bought the property in 1880 from the Tocqueville family, improved the water scenes. He multiplied the waterfalls, which henceforth faced each other on either side of the small valley. He transformed a torrent of water into a gentle current by installing a series of weirs which slowed down its progress to the sea. He also created a network of underground canals in order to control the water supplying the fountains.

A promenade rims the valley and overlooks the river which, in the summer, is bordered by white arum lilies. The soil is acidic, something rhododendrons are very partial to, and in the spring, their mauve flowers are omnipresent, invading the underwoods and even suffocating the new plantings. Pink, red, and white rhododendrons approach the château and mingle with azaleas, pieris, hydrangeas, and camellias. A few sequoias, planted by Hippolyte de Tocqueville as a tribute to American democracy, are still standing, but many fell in the terrible storm of October 1987, as unfortunately Nacqueville happened to be right in the path of the cyclone. Around twenty-six hundred trees were damaged and could not be saved. They were replaced with thirteen thousand beech, chestnut, American scarlet oak, alder, and Douglas pine saplings, the same species as those that remained.

If the weather is clear, one has a view over the river, the pond, and the sea from the White Bridge, which spans the valley. The fountains and the waterfalls dance. The giant leaves of the *Gunnera manicata* (which originates from warmer climes, as do the palm trees near the rhododendrons), create an aquatic and surprisingly exotic décor. However, the granite walls of the château and the back gates of the

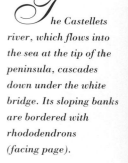

The Castellets river, which flows into the sea at the tip of the peninsula, cascades down under the white bridge. Its sloping banks are bordered with rhododendrons (facing page).

Cotentin manor houses are there to remind us of the typical Norman character of the area.

Plantbessin, a Garden and a Plant Nursery

The accessway leading to the Cotentin peninsula passes through a pretty farming region known as Le Bessin. Its damp, clayey soil is ideal for creating a water garden. Colette Sainte-Beuve's creation, which dates from the 1980s, is a garden within a garden. She set it in a structured, green, and floral décor composed of several garden rooms adjoining and acting as a showcase for her plant nursery.

a waterproof coating. Specially adapted containers were submerged in the basin to accommodate the plants, which were grouped by category to avoid entanglement. Each variety has a place according to its cultivation needs. For the water lilies, fifty or sixty centimeters' immersion was necessary, whereas for the pondeteria, the sagittaria (commonly known as arrowhead), the bullrushes, and the Japanese iris *I. laevigata*, platforms were submerged to a depth not exceeding five or ten centimeters.

A particular difficulty is encountered with this type of aquatic cultivation: how to prevent seaweed from proliferating? To combat this intruder, oxygenating plants were brought in, such as myriophyllum, elodea, and *Nymphoides pelata*, which help maintain an equilibrium.

In the gardens of Plantbessin two mixed borders in the purest English style combine all kinds of perennials: lupins, geraniums, Plantago nivalis, lychnis, lady's mantle (alchemilla), crambe, and meadow rue (thalictrum). Each flowerbed is punctuated by fastigiate yews.

The mixed borders are set in an enclosed green garden room and lead to a bench judiciously placed for enjoyment of the flowers and the geometric design of the ornamental pond (facing page).

The water garden at Plantbessin is beautiful because it is calm, green, and soothing. The border between nature and the garden is blurred. The water is at its best with the landscape reflected in it. To quote Gaston Bachelard: "The real eye of the land is water . . . In nature, it is water that sees, water that dreams." Water lilies float in the pond. Lady's mantle (Alchemilla mollis) flood the banks with their flowers, which look like green foam. Behind them goat's beard (Aruncus dioicus) raises ivory plumes; blue-green hostas (on the right), umbrella plants (in the foreground), and ligularia spread their large, opulent foliage; and delicate flowers such as primulas, irises, and pale yellow Sisyrinchium striatum (on the right) float in the air (following pages).

The water garden is both sober and opulent. Sober because of its simple design: a rectangular basin set in a similarly shaped garden room bordered by trees and shrubs. Opulent because the mixed borders spill over with flowering and foliage plants, attractively disposed in long clumps which give the impression of abundance. The garden is bathed in the white light particular to Normandy and which sets off the various aspects of volume, form, color, and texture of the foliage. This garden was created to meet two objectives: first to be pleasant to look at and second to display a good range of plants for visitors to the gardens and plant nursery, and to give them new ideas.

To create this water garden, a mechanical digger was brought in to make a gigantic pit. It was then reinforced and lined with concrete and

Generally speaking, once past the initial setup, aquatic plants (or those which thrive in a wet environment) are easy to live with. They proliferate and quickly form large splashes of color. Colette Sainte-Beuve has used both harmonizing and contrasting plant associations. She has blended spear-shaped with round or deep-cut foliage: rodgersia with hosta, irises with loosestrife (lysimachia), and primulas with lady's mantle (alchemilla). She likes soft colors and has favored white, yellow, and pink tones. The plants in this water garden are grouped by color and they harmonize perfectly with all the seasons, especially autumn with its gold or flame-colored foliage.

Spectacular plants can be grown in water gardens, such as gunnera or *Peltiphylum pelatatum*, known as the umbrella plant. Here

at Plantbessin, these plants are well-situated and can be admired immediately upon entering the garden, which tends to arouse curiosity and create an effect of surprise, whereas the plants with fine elongated foliage are planted at the opposite end to prolong the perspective and give an impression of distance.

The garden is surrounded by trees with soft, pointillist foliage which shrouds the pond in a gray and green mist. There are poplars and willows, notably the white willow (*Salix alba*) with its lovely, light, silvery leaves, or birches with barks which remain beautiful all year round, like the *Betula nigra* or *B. utilis* 'Jacquemontii', known as the West Himalayan birch.

With each visit different plants can be discovered, for new acquisitions are constantly being made. One can escape to the Japanese Garden, the Herb Garden, the Heather Garden, or the Mixed Border Garden to glean ideas for other types of décor.

The visitor has the impression of viewing many different scenes in a vast territory, whereas in fact the property only covers a quarter of an acre. Each garden room offers a surprising change of scenery, enchantment, and new ideas, but one is invariably drawn back to the freshness and beauty of the water garden.

A Water Garden Created by Russell Page

By proceeding north at the same remove from the coast, one reaches a region which is particularly rich in beautiful gardens. The garden of the Château du Pontrancart, in the Seine-Maritime department, is one of these marvels, whose floral exuberance we have already evoked (p. 36). Its water garden was designed around an ornamental lake by the celebrated English landscaper Russell Page, and its plant profusion renders it particularly attractive.

From the Louis XIII château, one overlooks both the water garden and the flower garden. The two are antithetical, for whereas the flower garden is structured, the water garden is of a more liberated design. The former adjoins the château, the latter melts into the Norman landscape.

Russell Page planted the peripheral trees and the perennials which adorn the banks. He applied the following principle: "Running water may involve a heightening of key so that both design and planting should suggest lightness and gaiety and movement; still water demands a quieter and more static treatment . . . trees, lawns and plantings should be arranged to accentuate their static qualities . . . I like to use water as a mirror laid out on the ground to give depth and interest by reflecting trees and sky" (*The Education of a Gardener*).

Over the years, the perennials, which are disposed in clumps, have acquired force and volume. They form domes which follow the meandering contours of the lake and which harmonize with the undulations of the nearby meadows. At the entrance a gigantic *Gunnera manicata* asserts itself and prevents one from seeing the whole garden in one glance.

If I were using water in a garden because I wanted water-side conditions, and moist soil for growing plants . . . I would want to handle my watercourses, pond or stream very discreetly." Russell Page's notion (from The Education of a Gardener) *is very characteristic of the spirit in which the garden at Pontrancart was created (below and facing page).*

The Japanese
bridge was the subject
of many of Monet's
paintings; he painted it
in 1900 before adding
the metal arch and
planting the wisteria
which was to cover it
(right).
A photo taken in 1921
shows Monet on this
bridge showing his
garden to Japanese
visitors, as he liked
doing with distinguished
guests such as Prime
Minister Clemenceau,
the art dealer Durand-
Ruel, or Georges
Truffaut, the
horticulturist.

The white
wisteria shades the
bridge like a voluptuous
lace curtain. This
variety of wisteria
flowers later than the
mauve one, and in some
years the flowering is
not abundant
(facing page).

Subsequently one discovers clumps of annuals whose flowers and foliage evoke the water theme. Giant-sized plants thrive here, such as the plume poppy *Macleaya cordata* with its gray-green foliage; tall gramineae rustling in the wind; the enormous, round, invading leaves of *Petasites japonicus* 'Giganteus'; rodgersia with their deep-cut leaves; or royal ferns (*Osmunda regalis*). They form massive patches on a similar scale to the imposing décor. Floral plants enliven the scene with their bright colors: daylilies (hemerocallis), purple loosestrife (*Lythrum salicaria*), yellow flags (*Iris pseudacorus*), ivory bugbane (cimicifuga), and white loosestrife (*Lysimachia clethroides*) with its copper-colored autumn foliage.

The water flows slowly in this peaceful haven, and the wind plays freely with the gleaming leaves.

The Water Lily Garden Created by Monet at Giverny

By following the Seine to Vernon, one can visit the famous water garden at Giverny and the water lily pond that Monet so loved to paint. In her publication entitled *Lumières*, Eva Figes invites us to participate in the making of a painting by Monet. She sets the scene in the garden and meticulously observes the artist: "The water lilies were now completely open and the shadows were less dense. At last the light was exactly how he wanted it and he therefore opened his box of colors . . . The bright light had accentuated the

fleshy parts of the leaves and flowers and the diversity of the contours. The smooth surface of the water was invaded by flowers and cushions of gleaming, black petals."

One knows of Monet's fascination for water and with what talent he composed his garden on the piece of land he acquired in 1893, on the other side of the Chemin du Roy. He created an ornamental pond and, drawing inspiration from his collection of Japanese prints, he built a Japanese-style bridge on which he fixed trellises to train wisteria. The water garden became a constant source of inspiration for him: "It took me some time to understand my water lilies . . . I had planted them simply for pleasure and cultivated them without thinking of painting them . . . And then suddenly the magic of my pond was revealed to me. I took my palette. Since then I have hardly ever used another model."

He had created this spot to favor meditation and contemplation, and he returned to it constantly. At all times of the day and in all seasons, the play of light and water and the beauty of this changing mirror reflecting the moving clouds constituted his staple diet. "Moreover, the effect varies constantly. Not only from one season to the next, but from one minute to the next, for the water flowers are far from being the only spectacle, in fact they are only the accompaniment. The principal motif is the *miroir d'eau*, whose aspect changes at every moment because of the patches of sky which are reflected in it and which suggest life and movement."

The water garden differs completely from the Clos Normand which we have already

The Water
Garden at Giverny in all
its glory, with its water
lilies, its yellow flags
(Iris pseudacorus),
and Japanese flags
(I. kaempferi) which
colonize the water and
the banks. Here too are
Petasites japonicus,
feathery ferns, and
willow branches which
weep in the water.
A Japanese bridge
structures the space
and adds a geometric
touch to the general
plant profusion
(following pages).

discovered in the chapter on flower gardens (p. 22). Its design is very free. A path follows the curves of the pond so that when strolling along it, one has the impression of being in a garden of vast dimensions. The décor is romantic, an invitation to daydream. The pond is planted with water lilies and along the edges with plants which thrive near water, such as Japanese flags (*Iris kaempferi*), blue Siberian flags (*I. sibirica*), and clumps of yellow flags (*I. pseudacorus*) and round-leafed petasites. Plants and shrubs which favor acid soil rise in tiers just beyond them, including azaleas, rhododendrons, and Solomon's seal (polygonatum), interspersed with mauve honesty (*Lunaria annua*) and the light trembling foliage of the equally mauve meadow rue (*Thalictrum aquilegifolium*). On the wide banks *Heracleum mantegazzianum* unfold their giant blooms next to arum lilies. The yellow clusters of a common laburnum (*L. anagyroides*) and the branches of a golden weeping willow (*Salix alba tristis*) bathe in the calm water.

Louis Vauxelles, the art critic, relates that when friends visited Monet, he took them first to his studio and almost immediately after to his pond, because "the water lilies close at five o'clock."

Early in the morning he picked a spot at the edge of the Water Garden to paint. One of the gardeners was responsible for the pond and of ridding it of anything which might cloud its limpidity, so that the gleaming foliage, the shadows, the evasive sun, and the moving clouds always would be reflected clearly in it.

The Dancing Waters
of the Château de Saint-Just

Saint-Just borders the Seine in the vicinity of Vernon. It is a charming, unspoiled country village possessing an authentic patina of tradition. The Château de Saint-Just towers above it and looks down upon the hillsides and the valley. A beautiful approachway bordered by century-old plane trees provides a foretaste of the park's main axis as it slopes up the hill to the château. Countless springs send water down this hill, transforming Saint-Just into a water garden which is both sophisticated and spontaneous.

The park surrounds the seventeenth-century château. It is the setting for terraces, a vast lawn which rises towards copses parted by French-style intersecting walks, and somewhat more romantic constructions such as the Pavillon de Sophie, a dairy, a Renaissance tomb, and a *glacière*.

Saint-Just is famous for its water scenes. The eternal springs which fill the *miroir d'eau* flow down from the woods in a myriad of small, perfectly straight stone canals, tracing linear patterns across the park. This water flows down a stepped cascade, transforms itself into a waterfall, then becalms itself in the ornamental lake, subsequently refreshing a drinking trough before watering the kitchen garden and the watercress bed. The canals, lake, cascade, and trough are prettily set off by recently acquired plants recommended by a young Norman landscape gardener named Denis Comont.

At Saint-Just, the grounds in the sloping wooded areas are crisscrossed by extraordinary canals, skillfully designed to conduct the water to the miroir d'eau (right and facing page).

Kitchen gardens in Normandy combine flowers, fruit, and vegetables. Green, blue, or red cabbages are both useful and decorative. They can be round, heart-shaped, or pointed; have wavy, curly, smooth, fleshy, or crinkled leaves; and reach maturity in the spring, autumn, or winter. Here they are to be seen in the kitchen garden at Limésy, a spectacular garden in the Caux region (following pages).

In summer the *miroir d'eau* is covered by water lilies. After the flowering, the leaves disappear underwater, providing shelter for the carp. Ducks glide between the yellow flowers and gray herons land gracefully on the banks.

The water circuits date from 1695 and we owe them to the Savary family, who were the proprietors at the time and who also planted the French-style gardens. They were subsequently redesigned in the English style in 1825 by Belguise, for the field marshal Suchet, duc d'Albufera.

The present proprietors, Monsieur and Madame Lalloz, are restoring the park. They replant saplings according to the original plans. They have studied in detail these ancient documents, which provide information on the daily life of the period and also on Victor Hugo's mother, Sophie Trébuchet, who once lived there.

As vice-president of the Association Régionale des Parcs et Jardins de Haute-Normandie, Monsieur Lalloz is striving to rehabilitate château gardens in Normandy.

GOURMET GARDENS

What is the definition of the French term *potager*? Traditionally it is a garden for *potagère* plants—those destined to be pot-boiled for soup—or, less specifically, a garden where vegetables and certain fruits are cultivated for consumption.

Everyone knows the amount of work involved in a kitchen garden: it requires methodical, meticulous, daily attention. Gustave Flaubert, whose works have their roots in Normandy, elucidates this task in *Bouvard and Pécuchet* when he describes Pécuchet working in a kitchen garden: "[he] bedded out the healthiest plants under bell-jars. He followed the precepts of the practiced gardener, respected the flowers, let the fruit set . . . He sprinkled them with water, aired them, removed the mist in the bell-jars with his handkerchief, and if clouds appeared in the sky he hastened to fetch the matting. It even prevented him from sleeping at night."

The Normans are fond of their food. They know how to reconcile utility and pleasure. They cultivate a large range of fruit and vegetables and prepare them *à la crème*, transforming simple produce into sought-after dishes which are the pride of the local inns.

Whether large or small, their kitchen gardens are always the object of attentive care. The Normans regularly combine flowers, fruit, and vegetables, which create welcoming, appetizing gardens. Traditionally the great kitchen gardens adjoined the châteaux.

This is the case with the Louis XIII château at Bosmelet in the Seine-Maritime. Today, Robert de Bosmelet is restoring the park and his wife, Laurence, is redesigning the kitchen garden according to the seventeenth-century plans. She is introducing a contemporary touch by planting it in the colors of the rainbow. First the blue tones of purple beans, green and purple cabbages, blue-green leeks, knapweed (centaurea), and blue statice. Then the yellow and orange tones of greenish yellow broccoli, pumpkins, nasturtiums, and yellow and orange poppies. These are followed by the pinks and reds of the irises, roses, purple knapweed, pale pink poppies, *Geranium psilostemon*, mauve potato plants, and Italian red lettuces. Lastly come white potato plants, green salad plants, ornamental variegated green and white cabbages, and white knapweed.

The rainbow theme is very elaborate and is treated with a great deal of subtlety. The site is perfect, as it is of exceptionally large dimensions, and so the spectrum can be admired in all its diversity.

Other more recent kitchen gardens also break away from the old traditions. They result from original designs by contemporary landscapers such as Pascal Cribier at Limésy, or Alain Richert, who created gardens in the Orne department which combined flowers, fruit, and vegetables.

The Norman orchards reflect the idyllic images of a rediscovered paradise, as regards both flowers and fruit. They are pleasant to look at, refreshing, moving, and full of delight. Norman apple farmers cultivate varieties of trees with charming names—names which the farmers protect. 'La Fertile de Falaise' and the 'Doux Veret de Carrouges' are cider apples, not to be confused with 'La Reinette de Bayeux' or 'La Reinette de Caux', which are eating apples. They can be sweet, sour, bitter, or acidic. Some are sensitive to vine mildew, canker, or bruising; others, on the contrary, are easy to cultivate.

Apple trees, as we all know, thrive in Normandy. Jean de La Varende knows them well: "[The apple tree] is the little prince, the heir apparent to the land of Normandy. It awaits a suitable décor and only arrives when everything is sufficiently majestic. It proves to be as capricious as a spoiled child. Whereas the pear trees all blossom at once, like disciplined soldiers . . . haughty apple trees don their apparel as and when they please. There are the precocious ones and there are the latecomers. They blossom for four weeks . . . However, there is a period of frenzy which only lasts a few days and when everything occurs at once; when the pear tree still gleams and the apple tree blossoms, when the grass becomes soft and emerald green, when the daisy is radiant and the buttercup yawns."

Due to the risk of frost, the stone-fruit trees such as peach, plum, or apricot are cultivated in greenhouses in the company of vines and fig trees, and so often blossom at odd times. They are planted at the foot of the wall on the outside of the greenhouse—with the trunk and branches trained into the shelter. It is a lovely sight which is enhanced by the arching vines and their pendant fruit. The grapes receive careful attention—the small clusters are removed to

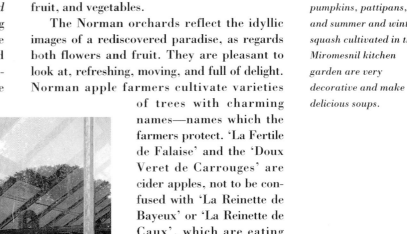

At Galleville, in the Caux region, the château kitchen garden is partitioned by color. This blue-green square is planted with beds of larkspur, carrots, zucchini, cabbages, and asparagus. An orchard stretches out behind the hedge (facing page).

The Cucurbita family: zucchini, pumpkins, pattipans, and summer and winter squash cultivated in the Miromesnil kitchen garden are very decorative and make delicious soups.

allow the larger ones to develop. Back outside, other fruit trees are planted in rows and trained on cords or against espaliers. Fruit is often grown in kitchen gardens and accompanies all kinds of vegetables, flowers, and aromatic herbs. Whether limited to small squares, or of more imposing dimensions, as is the case at Mont-Saint-Michel, all these kitchen gardens constitute a feast for the eye and the palate.

The Celebrated Kitchen Garden at the Château de Miromesnil

A typical example of traditional Norman kitchen gardens is to be found at Miromesnil,

The comte and comtesse de Vogüé purchased Miromesnil in 1938. Just after the renovation work was terminated, the Second World War broke out. Comtesse Simone de Vogüé began to cultivate her kitchen garden with a singular aim: that of feeding the family's children. She had an affinity for flowers and gardening and from the outset she combined vegetables and floral plants.

In the 1960s she opened the kitchen garden to the public and it proved to be a great success. She made regular progress, trying out the most promising plants and seeds, abandoning some and adding others. She bought supplies from abroad, consulted the best catalogues, and experimented with new harmonies, creating a spectacle lasting from spring to early winter.

Japanese anemones and geraniums add a bright splash of color to the typically Norman brickwork of this ancient outbuilding of the Château de Miromesnil (facing page).

The lupins and delphiniums at Miromesnil make wonderful bouquets. It is in the greenhouse where the preparations are made for the spectacle presented each season.

quite near Dieppe. This vast, walled kitchen garden, nestling among exceptionally majestic beeches, adjoins the pink, white, and gray Louis XIII château. It is renowned for its extensive choice of abundant, colorful vegetables, for its delphiniums, its clematis, and for its bouquets.

At the end of the sixteenth century, the lord of Miromesnil had a château built. He saw to it that the grounds were laid out in concord with the residence and the landscape. He planted clusters of beeches and framed the outlook with imposing perspectives. Later the property was surrounded by walls. They enclosed a courtyard, a kitchen garden, and a formal French-style garden which was subsequently redesigned in the more relaxed English style.

In the kitchen garden, work only begins in March or April when the soil is warm enough for sowing—otherwise the seeds do not come up. The first crops are ready in June: salad plants, French beans, and leeks. In July, turnips, celery, cabbages, and beets can be picked. August sees the crop of potatoes, carrots, and radishes; September brings zucchini, horseradishes, corn, and pumpkins. In November, Brussels sprouts make their appearance and endive arrives in time for Christmas.

Sweeter delicacies are mainly picked in summer, with strawberries in June and gooseberries, raspberries, and black currants in July. The apples and pears ripen in the early days of autumn.

One whole row in this garden is reserved for aromatic herbs, which include mint, sage,

In the Miromesnil kitchen garden near Dieppe, some walks are every bit as good as those along the best English mixed borders. They blend perennials such as phlox, hostas, and achillea with annuals like eschscholzia (following pages).

chives, thyme, vervaine, tarragon, angelica, dill, and basil, as well as most of the other herbs found in the best recipes.

The delphiniums are one of the crowning glories at Miromesnil. They accompany other flowers such as asters, phlox, cosmos, irises, carnations, veronica, and sweet peas, but one walk is specially devoted to them, a blue walk, perpendicular to the multicolored central avenue. The delphiniums do not like the wind, which manages to penetrate despite the walls. In order to reassure them, wire is stretched and they are provided with stakes. They have adopted the excellent habit of reflowering and thus perpetuating their incomparable blue tones, which range from pale to mauve and to almost black. They are ideal for bouquets.

Bouquets are, in fact, another Miromesnil specialty. This is the dominion of Odile—who also reigns over the kitchen. She is a born artist and possesses the talent of a great chef. She knows the best recipes and no-one can equal her special sole "à la Rosalie" or her strawberry cake—both prepared with freshly picked vegetables and fruit. Odile is also a born florist. Every two or three days at six o'clock in the morning, she changes the vases and composes her bouquets. These decorate the rooms which are open to the public. Large or small, but always extremely refined, the arrangements complement the vases, the décor, and the circumstances. Odile has a gift for blending seasonal flowers and she also likes using clematis, which she sets in a bowl in the center of the table.

As regards the clematis, her only problem is one of choice, for these plants are especially prolific at Miromesnil. They cover the brick walls of the kitchen garden and blend with the roses. Their single or double flowers bring even greater vivacity to the garden. 'Perle d'Azur', 'Nelly Moser', 'Prince Charles', 'The President', 'Duchess of Albany', or 'Vyvyan Penell' are like so many stars, with their tones of lavender or deep blue, purple, mauve or

deep violet, purplish red, or pure white.

A visit to Miromesnil enables one to glean good ideas and numerous are those who have drawn inspiration from it. Its beauty no doubt stems from its authentic utility, its magnificence, and its memories. Maupassant was born there, he who went into raptures over the main avenue: "the beeches were so tall that they seemed to reach the clouds." Miromesnil leaves the visitor with an impression of splendor and majesty and the kitchen garden radiates simplicity. All this is due to the particularly rich history of the domain, to the passage of time and the passions of those who have been connected with it.

A Contemporary Kitchen Garden on the Coast

This garden, laid out around a half-timbered Norman house near the coast, was created quite recently, just seven years ago in fact, by Louis Benech and Pascal Cribier. It is both beautiful and useful and combines vegetables, fruit trees, and flowers. It is an amalgam of new and traditional ideas, notably in the courtyard, where an ornamental pond replaces the traditional drinking troughs where animals quenched their thirst on the Norman farms.

The edges of the pond are punctuated by box cultivated in pots and on one side of it, Messiers Cribier and Benech have composed a green lawn with triangles of intermingled box. Typically Norman standard apple trees, very beautiful both when in bloom and bearing fruit, emerge from the boxwood and give this simple, light-hearted courtyard the aspect of an orchard.

Near the house, a small floral kitchen garden, enclosed by walls of yew, sets the scene for roses, dahlias, asters, and all kinds of useful plants such as *Artemisia absinthium* (a variety of wormwood), dill, tarragon, chard, chives, tomatoes, basil, and parsley. A little

farther on, a flowered embankment leads to an undulating orchard.

The soberness of the green carpet in the courtyard contrasts with the tapestry effect of the garden, which is itself embellished by very detailed compositions of countless varieties of gaily colored plants, which are brilliant against the clouds coming from the sea.

The Kitchen Garden and Floral Orchard at the Château de Galleville

Let us visit another traditional kitchen garden, that of the Château de Galleville, not far from

In 1702, the field marshal de Villars married Jeanne-Angélique de Varengeville who received Galleville and its dozen or so acres of land as her dowry. However, they both neglected the property; the field marshal was attracted by the splendors of Vaux-le-Vicomte, which he bought in 1705. His wife, who was very attached to Normandy, subsequently returned home and bequeathed the property to her son, who sold it. It changed hands several times again and fell into decay. The family of the marquis de Montault then took Galleville's destiny in hand, and from 1885 their descendants continually restored and improved the château and its grounds, just as the present proprietors, Monsieur and Madame Gillet, do today.

Not far from the coast, near Deauville, yew walls enclose this small, recently created kitchen garden. The central walk leads to a fountain covered with Virginia creeper and ivy and surrounded by bay laurels. The beds combine vegetables, flowers, and herbs.

Rouen. The vegetables are carefully lined up and grouped according to size, so that the plants progress in a tiered format starting with the shortest, a good idea which provides an overall view of the garden.

This kitchen garden is enclosed by walls and hedges and is very colorful. It forms a large rectangle in the park, which was redesigned in this century by the architect-landscaper Achille Duchêne. The garden is laid out parallel to the front and main courtyards and adjoins the seventeenth-century château, which is a model of equilibrium and harmony. Approached along an avenue bordered by monumental, majestic beeches, the château is built in the traditional pink, white, and gray brick and sandstone typically used in the Caux region.

The primary function of this kitchen garden is a practical one: the produce is destined for consumption. Carrots, celery, squash, fennel, asparagus, leeks, onions, cabbages, lettuces, and artichokes contribute to the menus, while the flowers fill the bouquets adorning all the rooms.

Even in the kitchen garden, Madame Gillet, who is vice-president of the Société des Amateurs de Jardins, takes pride in searching for color harmony and pretty scenes, introducing perfumes and creating perspectives, passageways, changes of style, and surprise effects. She followed the advice of Louis Benech, who suggested dividing the kitchen garden in two by means of a hornbeam canopy.

So what is still called the kitchen garden today is composed of a flower and vegetable garden and of a floral orchard, both ruled by paths crossing at right angles, which follow the main axes.

The flowers and vegetables are planted in large squares enclosed by box hedges and bordered by grassy walks. On entering, one finds squares containing low-growing flowers and vegetables such as bluish tough-leafed cabbages, purple beetroots, firm green salad plants, or carrots—neighboring with snapdragons, dwarf dahlias, or *Convolvulus minor*. The tall-growing flowers and vegetables are planted in the squares situated on the other side of the path: here tomatoes and corn meet delphiniums and sweet peas.

The orchard is reached by passing under the hornbeam canopy. There gravel paths

beauty of their blooms and foliage or for the delicacy of their bearing.

Then one passes from the shade into the sunshine, resulting in a complete change of atmosphere. Soft colors are replaced by bright ones, and the enclosed, secret garden gives way to an open, vivacious one. Gaura, gypsophila, cosmos, and Japanese anemones delicately spill over onto the path and accompany borders of the white annual, sweet alyssum (*A.* or *Lobularia maritima*), which, as its name indicates, diffuses a lasting, sweet perfume.

This gourmet garden is also a garden of color, atmosphere, and fragrance, of swarming bees and fluttering butterflies. A delight for the senses, it is not to be missed.

The paths in the Galleville kitchen garden form a cross and trace squares devoted to a specific color: white, yellow, red, and blue. In the red square one can distinguish dahlias, snapdragons (or antirrhinums), lettuces, tomatoes, and beets.

trace two perpendicular axes, the first bordered by pear trees, annuals, and perennials. The second leads to a white bench on one side, and on the other, to a green and white garden, designed by Louis Benech.

This is an intimate garden, fresh, pure, and serene. On three sides, yew ramparts are backed against walls and separated by white creepers such as the 'Marie Boisselot' or 'Huldine' clematis. Box parterres enclose combinations of white and green Christmas roses (helleborus), snow-in-summer (*Cerastium tomentosum*), and heather, which together produce a carpet effect. On one of the longer sides, a large "window" cut in a hornbeam hedgerow offers a view over an axis bordered by multicolored flowerbeds. Proliferating here are all kinds of plants which have been chosen for the

An Avant-garde Kitchen Garden Created by Pascal Cribier in the Caux Region

The land around Limésy has remained in the same family for more than five hundred years. Anne-Marie and Adalbert de Bagneux were married in the village church, where subsequently their children and grandchildren were christened. Adalbert de Bagneux thought a *potager* would be a good idea for their domain, La Coquetterie, but his wife did not desire to start a traditional, walled kitchen garden. She resorted to the talents of Pascal Cribier, who created an avant-garde kitchen garden whose upkeep is as simple as its design. It links the ancient, traditional Norman farm, which now

The kitchen garden and the orchard at Galleville are separated by a hornbeam canopy and united by a long flower border, which combines golden foliage and pink, gray, or pale green flowers. Farther on there is an apple orchard (following pages).

At the foot of the house, box balls growing between the paving stones form domes with simple, pure contours, which require minimum upkeep (facing page).

In this kitchen garden at La Coquetterie, the thirty-six squares designed by Pascal Cribier combine herbs, flowers, clipped ornamental shrubs, and vegetables. They are laid out in front of the stables of typically Norman design (above). On the other side of the house, around the swimming pool, Pascal Cribier conceived a long, wide border of perennial plants: one can distinguish pink phlox, the yellow spires of torch lilies (kniphofia), and promising-looking asters.

serves as the family residence, to the stables, which in winter still provide shelter for a large herd of cows.

Pascal Cribier laid out thirty-six beds, each measuring four square meters, and which are divided into three rows. They are surrounded by paving stones and separated by gravel paths. Each square is planted with a single variety of flower, herb, or vegetable. Some plants remain in the same place, others are moved or renewed, for as in all kitchen gardens, rotations are essential. It remains attractive all the year round due to the evergreen foliage of some of the plants. Thyme, garlic, sage, basil, chives, oregano, tarragon, and parsley, as well as salad plants, leeks, cabbages, artichokes, and lamb's-lettuce are cultivated for the greater delight of the family. Tomato plants even grow on the lawn under ovoid clipped hornbeams, which serve as living stakes. The garden is very sheltered and sunny, so the tomatoes ripen quickly and thrive.

Flowers also have their place and certain squares are reserved for them; especially blue flowers such as pansies, sages, or asters. Spring is greeted with white, pink, and yellow tulips. Santolina, forsythia, and broom, trimmed in box shapes, help to enliven the scene without breaking the geometric design.

Between the garden and the stables a wooden fence is decorated with a multitude of earthenware pots, each one containing a Jerusalem cherry (*Solanum pseudocapsicum*). Near the residence, next to a profusion of boxwood balls planted between the paving stones, one comes across a bench entwined with creepers, created by the sculptor Lalanne. Behind it, pretty plants such as camellias, hellebores, ferns, and hostas are cultivated in flowerpots.

In this kitchen garden Pascal Cribier has succeeded in reconciling utility and pleasure, passion and reason, tradition and modernity, the functional and the aesthetic. The atmosphere has become decidedly well-integrated here at La Coquetterie, where the sobriety of this garden and the splendor of the surrounding décor set each other off perfectly.

The early morning summer mist— on the point of lifting with the first rays of sun—spreads a blue veil over the kitchen garden, the family residence, and the stables (following pages).

Biological Cultivation in the Kitchen Garden at the Château de Villeray

Villeray and its kitchen garden are to be found on the other side of the Seine in the direction of the Perche region. It is overflowing with vegetables

cultivated according to both very old and very new methods, shunning chemical products. These vegetables possess a long-lost savor and people come from far afield to buy them.

Villeray is a perfect gem, with its steep paths winding up the hill, its ancient architecture, and traditional tiles covered with climbing roses, a village where even the smallest lilac-pink valerian is magnificent.

As regards the cultivation of the kitchen garden at the Château de Villeray, its proprietor, Madame Cruse, threw herself into an enthralling venture in which she invested a wealth of patience and energy.

The traditionally designed kitchen garden is to be found on the grounds of a Renaissance-style château, which has been in the Cruse family for several generations. It is a walled garden, prolonged by an orchard humming with beehives. The ancient orangery, which faces south towards large square beds, in winter houses oleanders (*Nerium oleander*), the squash crop, pots, bell-jars, and all kinds of tools, while on a table one will note a gardening calendar and the gardener's program.

The adventure began in Paris where Madame Cruse was attending lectures on horticulture. She learned how to prune, sow, cultivate, nourish, and treat. The result was a disaster, for in order to tend to her fruit trees, she was obliged to protect herself by wearing gloves, goggles, and a bonnet. She soon understood that if she were to continue to use chemicals, she would end up poisoning her kitchen garden. She changed course and discovered biological cultivation and the biodynamic method. This method, which is expounded in the thesis of the Austrian philosopher Rudolph Steiner (1861–1925), is very learned and complicated. It recommends the use of natural forces which vitalize the earth.

In keeping with these principles, Madame Cruse follows the gardening calendar established by Maria Thun, a German expert on biodynamics. Among other things, this calendar indicates when such and such a vegetable ought to be sown, according to the cycles of the moon. As the moon traces its ellipse around the earth, it passes in front of all the constellations and according to Maria Thun's theory, this is when—in given order—the leaves, flowers, fruit, or roots should be treated. If one contradicts this calendar just for fun, to test it, the results can be quite amusing. For example, if one plants radishes the

Madame Cruse, who is filled with exceptional energy and enthusiasm, has instilled new life into the kitchen garden at the Château de Villeray by converting to biological cultivation. This old-fashioned kitchen garden is very traditional. Rain water is collected in sunken tanks and old-style utensils and tools are used in the garden for the daily tasks.

The walled kitchen garden is vast. The vegetables and flowers are planted in neat rows. The vegetables are consumed by the family or sold at the market. The flowers are gathered for bouquets composed by Madame Cruse, which are always very original (facing page).

day when one is supposed to treat the leaves, they will produce far too much foliage.

For her kitchen garden, Madame Cruse uses organic fertilizer which she brews up herself. Manure from cows reared in biological farms constitutes the basis, to which she adds kitchen waste and decomposed leaves and weeds. She soaks it with a plant-based ingredient which activates decomposition and transforms this mixture into a sort of enriched compost. The result is that her soil is both remarkable and remarked upon by the local population.

In conformity with the biodynamic method, she treats her plants with herbal tea. She gathers reeds in the ditches and obtains an infusion which combats fungus. Against the cabbage pierid (a caterpillar which, before it transforms into a pretty yellow butterfly, is capable of destroying a crop overnight) she concocts a wormwood infusion. If a tree is stunted and the leaves turn yellow, she administers a dose of nettle tea, a sort of foliage compost which miraculously revives the vegetation. Additionally, her plants are skillfully associated so as to increase their defenses; for example, carrots are planted next to onions, which ward off the carrot flea.

Activity in the kitchen garden never ceases, work continues all the year round, and the production likewise. Thanks to this carefully applied method, the yield is high and the vegetables are succulent. People come from quite a distance to buy them and they are even sold at the local market.

One corner is reserved for flowers, for Madame Cruse composes notably beautiful bouquets. Here she mixes classic plants with leeks, radishes, and parsley—which she allows to go to seed and which are very decorative.

Climbing, botanical, Old Garden, and bush roses flower all over. They are supplied by her niece, who opened the plant nursery called the Roseraie de Berty. One can distinguish *Rosa moyesii* 'Geranium', *R. chinensis* 'Mutabilis', and the gnarled 'Roseraie de l'Haÿ' rosebush which thrives here. A little farther on, the old-fashioned, almost blue flowers of a *R.* 'Weichenblau' (also known as 'Blue Rambler') grace one wall.

All these flower garlands add to the softness of this place, which radiates a serene happiness in harmony with the village and the landscape. *Madame Cruse's indefatigable efforts to garden in an organically-sound, inventive way have resulted in plantings and produce acclaimed throughout the Norman countryside.*

The Kitchen Gardens of Mont-Saint-Michel

Mont-Saint-Michel is almost out of Normandy but not quite in Brittany. The site is spectacular and very moving. This is how Guy de Maupassant describes it: "The steep abbey, pushed right back, far from the earth, like a dream palace, incredibly strange and beautiful, looked almost black in the purple tones of the setting sun." The best time to go there is in October when it is less crowded and the vegetable and herb gardens, set in their stone showcase, reveal all their riches. At the outset these gardens were destined for the use of the community.

Five hundred steps have to be climbed to reach the Cloister Garden and the Garden of the Large Well right near the statue of Saint Michael, the Archangel. They have recently been restored, or rather, re-created, for although we are certain they existed in the past, no documents have been traced confirming their design, so they had to be reinterpreted.

The restoration of the Cloister Garden began in the early 1960s. Father de Senneville, advised by his uncle, the architect-land-scaper Jacques de Wailly, wanted the garden to be both useful and beautiful. He harmonized the colors, heights of the blooms, and the flowering periods, so that the plants would neither flower nor fade all at the same time.

In a very beautiful text which he entitled *Un Jardinier de Dieu*, he gives an allegorical account of this creation. He relates that he made "a very simple garden . . . of *simples* [medicinal plants]." He planted it in accordance with the requirements of the various brothers: medicinal herbs to cure the sick, decorative flowers for the cantor, and culinary herbs for the cook. He recounts that he was asked to create a "very simple garden, not according to his personal preferences, but a garden in obedience with the climate, exposure, colors, dimensions and dates of the flowerings. . . . It was harmony and divine proportions which were asked of him . . . rather than creativity . . ."

In the center, he designed a rectangular boxwood motif. Around it he decided to plant thirteen damask rosebushes, but they wilted and the blooms only lasted three days so he replaced them by modern, more resistant, hybrids. Around the lawn, he imagined a mixed border in gay colors. At each angle, he planted *Senecio maritima*, with its evergreen gray foliage, between clumps of yellow tickseed (coreopsis) which flower all summer. In the southern end, he planted peppermint, pink and red common (or cat's) valerian, irises, and hosta; in the west, achillea, sweet alyssum, and campanula; to the north, he planted thyme, chamomile, sage, *Artemisia absinthium*, silver *Stachys lanata*, and carnations; lastly for the east he chose lavender, saxifrage, and parsley.

Floral motifs carved into the stones above the pillars give the impression of prolonging the garden. They are representative of plants to be found in this region and one can distinguish bear's breeches (acanthus), rosebushes, blackberry, and raspberry bushes. They mingle with the ghosts of winemaking monks, for grapes used to grow in Normandy at one time.

The nearby Garden of the Large Well is even smaller. Its restoration was completed in 1990 and 1991. This garden is of definite historical interest since it figures in the plans of the abbey drawn up in 1701. Trellises are depicted on the walls and trees. A plan dating from 1775 indicates a crisscross design motif. Today, this little garden, situated at the foot of the abbey church's chevet (easternmost end), presents a checkerboard design. It is composed of eight boxwood squares, disposed around an ancient well adorned with white climbing roses. The squares are planted with traditional kitchen garden plants such as artichokes, cabbages, onions, leeks, rhubarb, celery, beans, and carrots. A hornbeam softens one of the angles. Two fastigiate yews lean against the chevet, near a chestnutwood gate surmounted by an arch entwined with honeysuckle.

A third garden is in the process of being restored. It dates from the fourteenth century and can be located on the eighteenth-century plan mentioned above. At that time this terraced garden was an orchard. Soon it will return to its initial vocation, as fruit trees will be planted with grass at their feet. Traditional varieties of apples have been chosen, such as 'La Calville', 'La Patte-de-Loup', or the small 'Pomme d'Api'. One day it will be possible to enjoy apples in complete serenity under the protection of Saint Michael, the Archangel.

At Villeray, as at Mont-Saint-Michel, cabbages are cultivated both for their nutritional and decorative value. Formerly they were also cultivated in the monks' gardens for their medicinal properties. Cato the Elder maintained that the ancient Romans were able to dispense with medicine for centuries, due to the consumption of cabbage.

The Garden of the Large Well, at the abbey of Mont-Saint-Michel. Visitors never see it like this, for Vincent Motte took this photo at sunrise. He was able to capture the rays of the sun filtering through the mist. A unique moment which only lasts a few seconds (facing page).

Domed Hydrangea macrophylla are easy to cultivate. Their colors vary from pink to blue depending on the variety and the quality of the soil. They rapidly form lovely, opulent clumps. The flowers become more beautiful as they fade. Hydrangeas are widespread in Normandy, as seen here in Corinne Mallet's property at Varengeville (following pages).

COLLECTORS'
GARDENS

Several eminent collectors figure among the inhabitants of Normandy, where the climate is particularly well-suited to the cultivation of a wide range of plants. A sort of competitive spirit and contagious enthusiasm exist between these inquiring-minded, fervent plantsmen and women. Princesse Greta Sturdza, creator and proprietor of the garden at Le Vasterival, is generally considered to be at the origin of this movement, and all are very grateful to her. Everyone is fascinated by this great lady and her garden, by her energy and her deep love of plants, which has encouraged the vocations of so many others. At the end of a conference on Le Vasterival, Philippe Gérard, president of the Association des Parcs botaniques de France, concluded with more or less the following words: "Each time I visit Princesse Sturdza's garden, I am not sure whether it encourages or discourages me." This is a typical reaction, for whereas Le Vasterival is a lesson in humility, it also enriches and awakens curiosity and one is fascinated by so much beauty. At this point, a tribute should also be paid to the late Dr. Favier, who died quite recently. He was a great collector who inherited the research work undertaken by his grandfather and who possessed one of the richest collections of foreign plants in France, which came from all over the world. His garden, La Roche Fauconnière, is situated in Cherbourg. Visiting the sea-rimmed property in his company was an unforgettable experience, so great was his love of flora. Like the princesse Sturdza, he has transmitted gardening fever to many of his visitors.

The Norman collectors form a sort of clan. Even if they amass different types of plants, they know and help each other, exchange ideas and specimens, belong to much the same associations, and use the same sources to enrich their collections. They all read a great deal, attend and give conferences, and frequent the same plant nurseries. They visit gardens both in France and abroad and welcome other collectors—who come from far and wide and who never hesitate to change their schedule to go see a rare specimen in the heart of the Norman countryside.

This is where the Conservatoire des Collections végétales spécialisées (CCVS)—whose mission consists of protecting France's plant heritage—comes in. They draw up a classified inventory of all the collections and encourage professionals and laypersons to become collectors. Normandy boasts several collections that have been approved by the CCVS, notably Madame d'Andlau's collection of daphne, Madame Buisson's and Corinne Mallet's hydrangeas, Dr. Evrard's collection of geraniums, and Martine Lemonnier's celebrated hellebore and meconopsis collections.

The Normans also take an interest in meadow flowers. The difference between a weed and a plant worthy of being displayed in a garden can be marginal, especially as some weeds are very decorative and moreover they are at the origin of a good number of hybridizations.

Jean-Claude Sellier, mayor of the charming commune of Mesnil-Durdent in the Seine-Maritime department, has established a rich botanical garden in front of a thatched cottage. He has named it the Jardin des Amouhoques, which is the French common name of the herb *Matricaria perforata*—commonly known in English as scentless mayweed—which proliferates in the Norman countryside. In this garden he has grouped all kinds of wild plants which are classified according to their environment. One bed is devoted to plants which favor damp ground, another to embankment plants, and others to meadow, harvest, and wayside flowers. They are all labeled with their Latin and common names and one comes across such terms as cranesbill, cow parsley (also designated cow weed, smooth chervil, cicely, keckson, mayweed, or white-weed); a variety of euphorbia known as devil's milk, wart grass, or sun spurge; followed by St. John's wort and hart's tongue.

Local wayside flowers are also labeled and one can find primroses, periwinkles, campion (also known as catch-fly), buttercups, and herb Robert (*Geranium robertianum*) interspersed with elders, dog rosebushes, blackthorns, brambles, and hazel bushes. A visit to this garden is particularly informative and the mayor's interesting initiative results in the discovery, appreciation, and consequently the protection of the wildflowers to be found in the Caux region.

The Jardin des Plantes in Caen also preserves and protects Norman plants, notably medicinal and other useful types, and at the Jardin des Plantes at Rouen one can study

175

At Le Vasterival, near Varengeville-sur-Mer, Princesse Sturdza has planted her flowerbeds with four levels of vegetation: bulbs (here daffodils) and ground-covering plants (wood anemones or heather); perennials; shrubs (Viburnum carlesii); and trees: maples, flowering cherries, and amelanchiers (facing page).

endemic Norman species. The arboretums at Harcourt and l'Etoile d'Andaines enable one to discover the different species of trees which are particularly adapted to the climate in Normandy. The plant heritage of this province is infinitely varied and constantly becoming richer as a result of the initiative of competent and enthusiastic collectors.

The Celebrated Collection of Rhododendrons at Le Vasterival

The exceptionally exuberant vegetation at Le Vasterival is the work of Princesse Sturdza, and remains the principal reference as far as Norman plant collections are concerned. In 1957, the prince and princesse, attracted by the clement climate, settled in Sainte-Marguerite-sur-Mer, not far from Varengeville. Here the garden benefits from the mild influence of the nearby sea.

If you were to ask the creator of this garden when is the best time to visit, she would recommend February, and indeed the show is astonishing in winter. This was her aim—attained thanks to her talent and competence, her enthusiasm and energy, and her love of plants.

Le Vasterival is a woodland garden of exceptional botanical wealth. It was inspired by Knightshayes in England, where, beyond the formal park, a garden is filled with plants which favor acidic soil, notably all kinds of species rhododendrons, and is carpeted with groundcover plants and rare, naturalized bulbs. Le Vasterival is in fact a series of collections within a collection, all in a very decorative style, for harmony was the leitmotif and the result is a veritable prose poem.

The design is very natural. It synchronizes with the gentle contours of the valleys and melts into the soft Norman landscape. There are meandering paths and undulating flowerbeds. Artificial ornaments are absent from the scene, as here one is too fond of nature to prevent it from expressing itself freely.

Each flowerbed is beautiful all the year round. Both the plants and the scenes are infinitely varied. First there are the pretty carpeting effects of creeping dogwood (*Cornus canadensis*), epimedium, tiarella (commonly known as foam-flowers), and lungwort (pulmonaria). These are interspersed with bulbs such as crocuses, snowdrops, fritillaria, colchicum, narcissus, tulips, and alliums. Following are all kinds of taller perennials, shrubs, and lastly trees—which play a protective role and whose

In winter, at Le Vasterival, heather forms a flowering carpet which creates a garden with a woodland atmosphere (above). Heather favors light, well-drained acidic soil and a sunny or partially shady exposure (below).

branches, foliage, bark, blossoms, berries, and fruit add to the beauty of the décor.

Le Vasterival is an all-year-round garden. In winter, the flowers are set off by a backdrop of evergreen trees and shrubs. Crocuses, Christmas roses (hellebores), alpine or winter heath (*Erica carnea*), camellias, witch hazel (hamamelis), skimmia, and a few early rhododendrons harmonize with the barks of birches and maples. It is in this season that the underwood is at its best. The forest is not dismal in February, nor indeed is Le Vasterival. Even in the depths of the cold, gray winter, the air here is heavy with the delicious fragrances of *Mahonia japonica* and wintersweet (*Chimonanthus praecox*).

Then spring arrives "and with it the great metamorphosis," as Princesse Sturdza describes it. "After the magic of winter follows another scene, both imposing and silent. All the flowers open out and rival each other in beauty. Spring is here and nonchalance is in the air." The small delicate blossoms of the flowering cherries set off the fleshier blooms of the crab apples and the magnolias. They are followed by azaleas and rhododendrons. The roses, the perennials, and above all the hydrangeas favor the summer. In the autumn the pointillist heather contrasts with the flat blooms of 'Autumn Joy' stonecrop (sedum) and with the round reddish heads of *Hydrangea serrata* 'Preziosa', and harmonizes with the flamboyant foliage of the maples (*Acer palmatum* 'Osakazuki'), with the berries of the hupeh rowan (*Sorbus hupenhensis*), and with the small 'Crittenden' crab apples.

On arrival one catches a glimpse of the Norman-style house which is set in a showcase of wild rhododendrons and surrounded by dark yew hedges. From there a soft, springy walk leads to the underwood where the vertical trunks of the maritime pines contrast with the rounded domes of the camellias and rhododendrons.

Le Vasterival is renowned for its collections of hellebores, skimmias, and hydrangeas, and the rhododendron collections are also unique. Their flowering is absolutely magnificent, lasting from February up until May. Some rhododendrons are very precocious and blossoms appear in the middle of winter, as with the *R. dauricum*, *R. racemosum*, *R. nobleanum*, and the 'Christmas Cheer' and 'Praecox' varieties. Others are remarkable for their blooms or foliage. The botanical varieties are delicately colored and very beautiful. *R. ungernii* has

At Le Vasterival, due to the proximity of the sea and tall protective trees, the early-flowering azaleas and rhododendrons do not suffer frost damage (above). A mossy, shady walk slopes down from the Norman-style house to an underwood inhabited by species rhododendrons (below).

A symphony in green in a valley where a wedding-cake tree (Cornus controversa 'Variegata') spreads horizontal branches adorned with delicate, variegated foliage (facing page).

The satin poppies (Meconopsis napaulensis) cultivated by Martine Lemonnier originate from Nepal and Sichuan. They flower in June, July, and August. The first flowerings appear at the top of the plant and gradually progress down the stem. On one plant it is possible to see seed pods, fully blown flowers, and buds all at the same time, which explains the length of the flowerings (facing page).

pale pink flowers and gray, almost silver leaves. The 'Polar Bear' is a late-flowering variety and blooms only appear in August.

The magnolias are also one of the crowning glories of Le Vasterival. Certain rare specimens such as *M. dawsoniana* bear flowers of an exceptionally beautiful size and color. When she planted it, Princesse Sturdza knew that she would have to wait sixteen years for the first flower, but what a reward! *M. sprengeri* var. *diva* also bears enormous pink flowers. *M. cylindrica* has a very beautiful bearing and its flowers are large and white. The *M. tripetala* is late-flowering. They are all very noble and graceful. Above all, the Varengeville climate suits them perfectly, as they require mildness and humidity.

The richness of the soil at Le Vasterival is not a gift of nature. At the outset the soil was acidic. The life force of this garden resides in the use of mulch—a mixture of fertilizer, leaf mold, and pine needles—which is nourishing and protective, retains moisture, and prevents weeds from proliferating.

A profusion of wild plants can be seen in the flowerbeds and one can distinguish violets, heather, ferns, Solomon's seal (polygonatum), and foxgloves, but here at Le Vasterival these wild flowers are larger, stronger, and more beautiful than those in the field. As one of Princesse Sturdza's friends remarked: "La princesse sent et pressent les plantes" ("The princesse both scents and has a sense for plants"). Gardening requires savoir-faire and the eye of an artist, an alchemy which is at the heart of Le Vasterival's magic.

The Hellebores
and the Himalayan Plants in
the Bellevue Gardens

Now we move inland, but still in the Caux region, where between Dieppe and Rouen, at Beaumont-le-Hareng, one comes to a plant nursery and a garden: La Pépinière du Coudray and Les Jardins de Bellevue. They belong to Monsieur and Madame Lemonnier and harbor two magnificent collections.

Martine Lemonnier entertains a winter and a summer preoccupation—she loves both hellebores and Himalayan specimens such as primulas and

meconopsis. Her husband and children are as fervent as she is. Their passionate search for rare varieties led them to create this garden and plant nursery.

It all began with reading and visits to other gardens. Le Vasterival and the Edinburgh Botanical Garden stood out as models, as they had permitted our hosts to discover certain plants of a totally unexpected beauty. They were fascinated by the richness of the hellebores, which, in winter, illuminate even the barest of gardens, and also by the meconopsis and its heavenly blue tones, which no other plant can equal.

Today the hellebores are planted in close-set rows, in a garden divided up in the fashion of a *potager*. They can be admired in the midst of numerous perennials which are disposed so as to facilitate propagation. Certain hellebores in containers can be found in the greenhouses, where they can be more easily observed, and in February great masses of blooms offer a spectacular display. White, pink, purple, green, ivory, pale yellow, violet, almost blue or black, pure or dotted, with double or triple blooms, the panoply is absolutely magnificent and one hardly knows which ones to look at first.

The hellebore is an invaluable plant in gardens. No doubt if it flowered at a different season, it might attract less attention, but it so happens that its reign commences in the first days of winter and lasts until May. The flowers are imposing and the foliage is of exceptional beauty. The deep green, strong leaves, slightly or deeply divided, are present all the year round and few things are more beautiful than a frost-covered hellebore.

Helleborus niger (or Christmas roses) are of course the best known of the hellebores. They are pure and radiant, but not always very docile, whereas the Corsican hellebores (*H. corsicus*), or the oriental hellebores (*H. orientalis*) have no particular susceptibilities. One thing that these plants detest, however, is being moved. They need ordinary soil and a lengthy acclimatization period.

The hellebores close to the Lemonniers' Norman-style house are planted between small boxwood hedges which set off the flowers and their foliage. She has a preference for the purple-dotted white 'Hélène' and the snow-white 'Lucie' varieties of

Meconopsis × sarsonsii, with their ivory flowers and golden stamens, are extremely rare. They flower in May and June.

oriental hellebores. She mingles them with winter- and spring-flowering plants: all kinds of bulbs such as snowdrops, cyclamen, crocus, and fritillaria; and with spring flowers like lungwort (pulmonaria) and wood anemones. They are also in the company of winter-flowering shrubs such as *Viburnum bodnantense*, honeysuckle (*Lonicera fragrantissima*), wintersweet (*Chimonanthus praecox*), *Corylopsis pauciflora*, and winter jasmine (*Jasminum nudiflorum*). These hellebores recently have been registered as a classified collection by the CCVS.

As the seasons advance, the Himalayan plants take over, that is to say Asiatic primulas, meconopsis, and cardiocrinum. They are as happy under the skies of Normandy as they

are under those of the Himalayas or Scotland, as they favor cool, shady sites.

Martine Lemonnier has assembled about forty varieties of Asiatic primulas. She is very fond of the candelabra family whose white, orangeish, yellow, pink, or deep purple flowers are borne in tiered whorls, an example of which is the beautiful, fragrant, lemon-yellow *P. helodoxa*; but her preference goes to the 'Insriach Hybrid' primula, with its eight-tiered whorls of apricot-colored flowers, which requires a sunny exposure and blends perfectly with the brickwork of her Norman residence.

Then there are the meconopsis poppies growing in the underwood, like a great wave of delicate, luminous, silky blue—irresistible to the eye.

Here at Bellevue there are thirty-five species and varieties of meconopsis, a gathering which has also been classified as a national collection by the CCVS. Most of these poppies originate from the Himalayas. They favor shade, a cool (preferably woodland) setting, and an acidic soil which is well-drained and well-fertilized.

Meconopsis betonicifolia, *M. grandis*, or *M.* × *sheldonii* are quite unforgettable. *M. napaulensis*, known as the satin poppy, is another of nature's masterpieces with its velvety, silver foliage and its clusters of pale yellow flowers.

Cardiocrinum, originating from Tibet and from Hunan in China, are underwood bulbs which grow to resemble yards-tall lilies. Their

trumpet-shaped blooms are white, tinged with purple on the inside, and very fragrant. Seven years are needed before the first flowerings are obtained.

All these plants start out in the Coudray nursery, which is integrated in the Bellevue gardens. Yew or beech hedges serve to protect and delimit the garden rooms. In an area which resembles a kitchen garden, with a central path separating two sections divided into beds, Martine Lemonnier cultivates propagation plants for her collections. A little farther on she has created an experimental garden, where she has assembled such curiosities as green-flowered roses or unusual colored gramineae.

An arboretum planted with nothofagus, Persian ironwood (*Parrotia persica*), dogwood

(cornus), and magnolias surrounds the garden. With its interplay of foliage, branches, and barks, it serves as a magnificent backdrop for these precious collections.

Near Rouen, Hundreds of Geraniums from All Over the World

The Caux region is without doubt one of the richest areas in Normandy as far as plant collections are concerned. Some three hundred varieties of geraniums, for example, are assembled at the garden of Dr. Evrard, called Les Forrières-du-Bosc.

It all started during his military service, which bored him profoundly. To break the monotony, he bought a magazine on perennial plants, which proved to be a revelation and the beginning of a passion. Subsequently Dr. Evrard and his wife bought a charming, half-timbered Norman house at Saint-Jean-du-Cardonnay, near Rouen, surrounded by an unkempt garden. That was ten years ago. They cleaned up the plot of land; cleared the sequoias, Scots pines, conifers, and deodar cedar; and started the plantings (about which, in fact, they were not very knowledgeable). England attracted them and they visited the gardens at Sissinghurst, Great Comp in Kent, and Shefield Park in Sussex, where they gleaned the idea for a heather garden. Then they tried out perennials, notably geraniums,

of which, funnily enough, they were only moderately fond. It was more of a marriage of convenience: the Evrards simply found them interesting and easy to cultivate in this region. And then, quite naturally and spontaneously, collector spirit got the better of the lord of the manor. Multiple visits to the French plant nurseries followed, and he soon found himself the proud possessor of about a hundred varieties. Then, with new discoveries and occasional foreign infusions, he gradually increased his collection. Today he possesses 334 varieties of geraniums, which have been approved as a registered collection by the CCVS. He has become a specialist on geraniums and he regularly exchanges ideas and specimens with his colleagues.

He never goes into his garden without a magnifying glass, an indispensable precision instrument for the expert who wishes to identify certain varieties with certitude. Novelties can in fact come up in the garden one fine day, the result of crossings due to the miracle of nature and the intervention of the bees. One therefore needs to be able to observe them on the spot, meticulously. Much experience is needed to distinguish geraniums, for the differences between them are subtle. They always have five petals, but these petals can overlap or be separate, the extremity can be notched or rounded. They can be plain-colored or veined, the flowers can bear discreet or prominent stamens. They can also be identified by their method of seed ejection, by the implantation of the leaves, or by the manner in which the blooms are grouped on the stem.

The colors of perennial geraniums are very attractive. They vary from white to almost black, from pink to mauve, blue, red, violet, and purple. Flowerings take place from spring to autumn depending on the varieties. Some are remontant, others only start blooming in September or October—like the *G. wlassovianum* with its intense deep blue blooms and its flamboyant foliage at the end of the season. Certain geraniums are native to France. This is the case with *G. robertianum*, *G. sylvaticum*, and *G. nodosum*, but others originate from South Africa or Madeira, from China or Australia. One has to cheat with Normandy and create microclimates to suit them. Depending on the variety, they prefer shade or sun, clayey or rocky soil, damp or dry atmospheres.

nonstop, from sunrise to sunset. When it gets dark they move into the greenhouse. Dr. Evrard spends three or four hours a day on his collection. He gardens, of course, but he also keeps up a regular correspondence with other collectors; takes photos; gathers seeds, sows, and propagates; and makes studies armed with magnifying glass, dictionary, specialized documentation, and notebook. All the plants growing in the garden are recorded in detail on the computer.

The garden spreads around the house. It is not a garden *à la française* and it is not an English-style garden either. As a friend once said, it is a "Franglais" garden. Certain parts of it are structured and others are of a more liberated design. One will find geometric

The 'Ann Folkard' geranium (G. procurrens × G. psilostemon) is combined with Alchemilla mollis, or lady's mantle (facing page).

In Dr. Evrard's garden, the geranium flowerings succeed each other throughout the summer months: G. × oxonianum 'Lady Moore' (left), and G. 'Patricia', which is the result of the crossing of G. endressii and G. psilostemon (right).

Not all geraniums are perennial. Some are annual or biennial and self-sow easily, to the point of becoming invasive. Some have aromatic foliage like the *G. macrorrhizum*, others have large or variegated leaves bordered with brown or yellow. The majority bear single flowers, but some double-flower varieties do exist.

The more one enriches one's collection, the more one turns towards the botanical species, for they possess an authenticity which obviously cannot exist in the case of hybrids. Species geraniums are difficult to find. The best method is to become a plant hunter and track them down in their country of origin. Dr. Evrard is very enthusiastic about this sort of adventure.

Les Forrières-du-Bosc is a very well-kept garden. On weekends, the owners work at it

flowerbeds disposed around a garden pavilion or a stone ornament, or beds with sinuous contours in the heather garden and near the water garden. The geraniums are grouped by family and planted in clumps somewhat reminiscent of display shelves. Each one is in its place, they do not hamper each other, and all are labeled. In other parts of the garden where the collection spirit gives way to a more decorative style, perennials can be seen blending with flowering shrubs.

In 1993, this garden of rare species was awarded the Bonpland Prize by the Société Nationale d'Horticulture de France, to encourage Dr. Evrard and his wife to keep up their work. They are inhabited by ineradicable enthusiasm and energy, and form countless projects which augur a radiant future for

their garden. Les Forrières-du-Bosc resembles those well-kept English gardens which welcome the visitors in all simplicity, for the love of plants, and the desire to share it with the like-minded.

One Hundred and Thirty Varieties of Hydrangeas in a Small Garden

In the same village of Saint-Jean-du-Cardonnay near Rouen, a remarkable collection of hydrangeas can be admired in a small garden named Le Thuit Saint-Jean.

The garden immediately reveals all its special qualities. The plants serve as a bouquet of welcome in the manner of cottage gardens, and have been chosen and charmingly disposed by an expert. Masses of flowering creepers mingle with shrubs in a tangled, informal hedgerow. Roses, clematis, and honeysuckle trace garlands along a picturesque fence backed against trees or shrubs such as a *Salix sachalinensis* 'Sekka' willow or a 'Rose Glow' berberis. Among the roses one can distinguish a 'Sainte-Vierge'—or perhaps it is an 'Albéric Barbier', since they are very similar. Be that as it may, cuttings are made between 15 August and 8 September, as the beautiful glossy foliage becomes invading and almost-white flowers appear. It is in good company and blends with a *Clematis montana* 'Tetrarose'; a *C. tangutica* with its remarkable, bright yellow lantern-shaped flowers and silver fruit; and with the discreet, fragrant, violet-colored flowers of a chocolate vine (*Akebia quinata*).

Collection fever has always existed at Le Thuit Saint-Jean. The proprietor, Madame Buisson, a collector to the core, first satisfied this passion with objects before extending it to plants. One day she was captivated by the photo of a *Hydrangea aspera* subsp. *villosa* in a gardening magazine, which resulted in a veritable treasure hunt. Madame Buisson called her husband into this endless quest and together they visit the best nurseries and meet eminent French or foreign specialists.

The Norman climate facilitates their hydrangea-mania, as these plants do not like heat or sun and some detest the cold. If by chance the summer proves torrid, Madame Buisson goes as far as protecting her favorite plants with parasols. They deserve it, of course, because this hydrangea collection is now approved by the CCVS. Today Le Thuit Saint-Jean boasts one hundred and thirty varieties. The first group is composed of arborescent hydrangeas originating from America. All bear domed or flattened white flower heads, which gradually turn to a greenish shade. Their foliage is reminiscent of lindens. Then comes the *Hydrangea macrophylla* family, again with domed or flat flower heads, of which 'Mousseline' with its bluish flowers, underplanted with a carpet of epimedium and *Geranium macrorrhizum*, is a fine example. They are followed by *H. aspera* varieties, which bear very beautiful, rough or velvety leaves. Monsieur and Madame Buisson can also claim three varieties of *H. petiolaris*, which are climbing plants, the only ones they are able to cultivate as the other varieties are not hardy. Next one can distinguish *H. heteromalla* varieties. These flower as early as the end of April, if there is no frost damage, and regularly attain a height of fifteen feet. The flowers are white and turn pink at the end of the summer. The next group consists of the *H. paniculata* with their distinctive conical panicles of white flowers in summer, which also turn pink later in the season. The last group represented is that of the *H. quercifolia*, or oak-leafed hydrangea, with its double or triple flowers.

The show which is staged here in this garden continues without interruption from spring to autumn. The colors evolve with the seasons and change from one year to the next depending on the weather conditions. The flower heads are pink, white, mauve, purple, or violet. Some varieties fade very prettily and make elegant dried bouquets, like the *H. macrophylla* 'Intermezzo' or 'Altona' varieties. For this purpose, they should be put in water which is allowed to evaporate and gradually the petals become as brittle as paper, but keep their beautiful colors. A visit to Le Thuit Saint-Jean is very instructive. One can study the hydrangea family tree, which has its roots in China and Japan, and furthermore follow an exceptionally interesting, detailed commentary which

The small garden at Le Thuit Saint-Jean harbors a beautiful collection of hydrangeas. Here one can see assembled: H. petiolaris (on the left, climbing up the wall of the house), H. arborescens (below, with flattened heads), and H. macrophylla 'Sunset', very characteristic of its species (center). At the top left one can distinguish the domed heads of H. macrophylla 'Générale Vicomtesse de Vibraye' and at the top right, H. paniculata 'Unique' (facing page).

At Le Thuit Saint-Jean, this Hydrangea macrophylla is labeled under the name 'Altona'.

enables one to discover the special qualities that are embodied in each plant.

A Collection of Hydrangeas at Varengeville

At the end of July, with the hydrangeas in bloom, the garden at Varengeville is perfectly glorious. Due to the proximity of the sea, the light shimmers and creates special reflections, which illuminate the hydrangeas in a particularly beautiful way.

The garden is quite an adventure, for Corinne Mallet has assembled a collection of hydrangeas which has been approved as a registered collection by the CCVS. Started in 1983, it is exceptionally rich. Madame Mallet was fascinated by hydrangeas, whose foliage is as beautiful as the flowers, and which remain beautiful with the passing seasons.

It varies from year to year, but in general the first buds open at the end of June and certain species bear flowers until the first frosts. The majority of these shrubs are deciduous, which Madame Mallet prefers to evergreens, because even with the naked eye, one can literally see them grow and

evolve. She started looking feverishly for new varieties and she is as insatiable as her quest is endless. Not only did she undertake plant research, but she also assembled a large quantity of documents. Unfortunately the information was confusing, so she started taking notes to put some order to her observations and in 1992 this resulted in a book—the book she had been looking for and had never found. It is entitled *Hortensias et autres hydrangéas*. She wrote it with her husband Robert Mallet, Guillaume Mallet's grandson, and with Harry Van Trier, the curator of the Kalmthout Arboretum. Since then she has published a second volume on hydrangeas.

The garden dates from 1990; before that the hydrangeas were planted in a provisional site until the Shamrock Garden was ready for them (so named in memory of a trip to Ireland and its incomparable verdure).

Here the domed flower heads mingle with the flattened ones, setting off white, blue, or pink waves in the orchard. Corinne Mallet knows the name of each, their particularities and origin, their cultivation requirements, and family tree. To differentiate one from another, it is sometimes necessary to observe them under the microscope, and a very good memory is needed to identify them properly.

Hydrangea macrophylla 'Gartenban Direktor Kuhnert' "is only at its best when cultivated in acidic soil," explains Corinne Mallet in the book which she has devoted to this genus. The flowering, which is not very abundant, begins in mid-July and finishes by late August, at which time it takes on a purple-and-blue tone which is quite remarkable (above).

Some are arrayed against a hornbeam hedge which provides shade in the morning. *Hydrangea paniculata*, with its conical panicles of white flowers which, with time, turn to pink, adorns a long border and is interspersed with other shrubs, such as Japanese snowball trees (*Vibernum plicatum*), elders (*Sambucus nigra* 'Purpurea'), and the silver foliage of hippophae (sea buckthorn). Corinne Mallet advocates grouping the *Hydrangea paniculata* varieties together, as they have their own particularities. Her favorites are the 'Unique' and 'Burgundy Lace', which also take on a pink blush with the passage of time.

Under the apple trees, she has assembled the *Hydrangea macrophylla*. They are legion and bear round flower heads. She recommends 'Blue Deckel', a most prolific flowerer, and 'Rosea' or 'Heinrich Seidel', which take on lovely pink, blue, mauve, or purple tones when fading and are suitable for dried bouquets. 'Madame Emile Moullière' which lends itself to flowerpot cultivation, is yet another good investment, with its abundant flowers which are white at the outset, then green, and finally pink.

This is a garden with international constituents. In order to enrich her collection, Corinne Mallet

made the rounds of the European plant nurseries. She traveled in England, Belgium, Germany, Holland, and Switzerland, where she made contact with nursery experts and collectors. By following up all the information, she managed to find forgotten varieties. She showed much curiosity and tenacity when it was a question of saving a genus or a cultivar.

She made two trips to Japan, which she regarded as pilgrimages. In order to botanize and be able to bring back native plants, she braved the typhoons which carried off her tent, pitched at the foot of Mount Fuji. She increased her collection, however, from thirteen to sixteen species, as she was able to bring back cuttings (botanizing is permitted there as long as one does not touch the roots). In Japan she met Dr. Yamamoto, the world authority on hydrangeas, who possesses a minute garden and cultivates his hydrangeas in flowerpots, like bonsais, on three levels.

Madame Mallet's hydrangeas also come from China, Sumatra, Korea, Java, the Philippines, and South America. They are now all well-acclimatized to her garden. These flowers united in Normandy in complete accord. They create color harmonies of a rare beauty which blend perfectly with the skies of Varengeville, so dear to Monet and Braque.

Hydrangea macrophylla 'Buntspecht'. These hydrangeas, with flattened heads known as lacecaps, bear peripheral flowers which are large and sterile.

Vauville, a Subtropical Garden at the Tip of the Cotentin Peninsula

In a windswept site warmed by the Gulf Stream, an astonishing collection of plants from the southern hemisphere awaits.

The Vauville manor garden is full of surprises. It owes its originality to the climate, to its plants, and to its design. Situated at the tip of the Cotentin, it benefits from an exceptionally mild climate, for here the temperatures rarely descend below freezing. This enables plants which normally must be protected or sheltered to be cultivated in open ground. This

The latter offer spectacular effects in the form of sudden views onto the coastal meadowlands and the sea. Invisible but audible, it suddenly appears between a wall of escallonia and a rampart of *Gunnera manicata*, whose gigantic leaves could hide an elephant.

Eric Pellerin and his wife started creating this subtropical garden in 1947, around the manor house which has always been in the family. This little fortress is situated near the village church and from the tower one has a view over the typically Norman, verdant pasturelands and, in fine weather, one can see out to Alderney Island. The tower dates from the twelfth century, the other outbuildings from the sixteenth and seventeenth centuries, and the dovecote was built in 1732.

*In the gardens at Vauville at the tip of the Cotentin peninsula, a wall near the château bedecked with 'American Pillar' roses acts as a windbreak. All the plants in this garden (*Mimosa dealbata *in the foreground on the left, New Zealand cabbage palms [*Cordyline australis*] behind them on the left, and tree mallows [*Lavatera olbia*] behind the arch) are very frost tender.*

*Spanish gorse (*Genista hispanica*) on the left; white-flowering Hebe longifolia in the center; senecio, tree mallow (lavatera), fuchsia, and eucalyptus on the right (facing page).*

Very architectural plants structure the area: Echium wildpretii, from the Canary Islands, with their long vertical spires; the very rare, spiky Dasylirion acrotrichum in the center; and foxgloves. These contrast with the more diffuse flowers and foliage of Senecio lineraria in the right foreground and the pink flowers of tree mallow (following pages).

universe, created by Eric and Nicole Pellerin, is reminiscent of the experience of Osgood Mackenzie at Inverewe in the north of Scotland and that of Augustus Smith, in the last century, at Tresco, off the coast of Cornwall, who both planted very unusual vegetation for these latitudes.

There is, however, a dark side, for while the temperatures are very clement, the wind is terrible. When crossing the arid, sandy moors which slope down to the village and the sea, one comes across vegetation tormented and tortured due to the merciless wind. It is for this reason that the Vauville garden is ridged by windbreaks. Informal walls of greenery and hedges of natural contour serve as screens to stop the wind. They also partition the enclosures, which are linked by simple walkways.

The botanical garden is laid out in the shelter of the manor's moats. Massive plantings of gray-green eucalyptus, escallonia (which can measure several yards in height), cypresses, New Zealand cabbage palms (*Cordyline australis*), the *Eryngium pandanifolium* variety of sea holly, gynerium (which is very spectacular when densely planted), and giant New Zealand flax (*Phormium tenax*) all evince the originality of this garden. The walls of New Zealand flax, with their impressive sword-shaped leaves and which today attain a height of ten feet, were obtained from a modest tuft, formerly planted in the courtyard, which Eric Pellerin decided to divide.

These plants are very sensitive to the cold, but they prosper in Vauville and protect other frost-tender plants like arum lilies, agapanthus,

𝒯he Tasmanian snow gum (Eucalyptus coccifera) can survive at 10° F in well-drained soil (above). Tree mallow originates from the Mediterranean regions, is very easy to cultivate, and flowers profusely all summer (below).

wormwood, bear's breeches (acanthus), palms, and camellias; or again the pink-flowering *Amaryllis belladonna* and delicate alstroemeria, dahlias which remain in open ground both in summer and winter, hollyhocks (alcea), dimorphoteca (commonly called African daisy or Cape marigold); and *Echium pininana* and *E. fastuosum*, with their evergreen foliage and spikes of giant, bright blue blooms, which originate from Madeira. The plant screens also protect the arborescent ferns (*Dicksonia antarctica*) and abutilons

(which in most other regions cannot survive outdoors in winter), as well as Mediterranean plants such as mimosa, rock roses (cistus), agaves, banana trees, and a red-flowering callistemon (commonly known as bottlebrush because of its cylindrical clusters of flowers).

These plants come from all over the world and create an astonishing, luxuriant, subtropical décor which was designated a historical monument in 1992. This garden is lucky, for its creators have succeeded in transmitting their passion to their children, Marie-Noëlle

*The spires
of bear's breeches
(Acanthus mollis) can be
seen dodging between
the gray foliage and
yellow flowers of
Senecio pulcher on the
left and rosemary
(Rosmarinus officinalis
'Prostratus'
(above left).
In summer, Cistus
'Silver Pink' produces
pink flowers and
evergreen foliage
(above right).*

*The delightful
blue flowers of an
evergreen Ceanothus
burkwoodii mingle with
perovskia (on the left in
the foreground), whose
lavender blue spires will
then take over, and with
Cineraria × hybrida
(below).*

*A
seventeenth-century
dovecote located
in the Auge region
(page 200).
Rhododendrons
at Les Moutiers
(page 201).*

and Guillaume Pellerin, and his wife, Cléophée. Guillaume Pellerin collects ancient garden implements, which he soon hopes to be able to exhibit in a museum. He is fascinated by landscape gardening and entered this profession after giving advice on this subject to his neighbor Jacques Prévert. Marie-Noëlle, Cléophée, and Guillaume Pellerin put their heart and soul into Vauville and the garden is constantly enriched by new plants.

Whether they be historic or contemporary, large or small, public or private, the gardens of Normandy constitute a rich plant heritage, of which the regional authorities are justly proud, for they attach great importance to the garden world in this day and age. The Norman plantsmen and women entertain great projects and, spurred on by a contagious enthusiasm, they unite their efforts to ensure the restoration and preservation of this wealth of color and fragrance. Through their magnificent gardens, they transmit to others the desire to follow in their footsteps and experience the joy of creating beauty.

VISITOR'S GUIDE

ADDRESSES FOR GARDEN LOVERS

Normandy harbors a vast quantity of gardens which evoke the past, the present, and the future of the gardening art. Many are open to the public. Most of the sites listed below are described or mentioned in this book; for those who wish to visit other parks and gardens open to the public we have added a few that are well worth a visit. The bibliography provides references to the best guidebooks.

In addition to the gardens themselves, this section lists landscape gardeners working in Normandy, associations run by devoted amateurs who are eager to help visitors, lists of nurseries and garden shops, a bibliography, information regarding itineraries for visiting Normandy, and accommodations where one can stay in a charming floral environment. In short, a guide for furthering knowledge and for pleasurable visits.

Since opening hours and conditions vary from one year and from one season to the next, it is advisable to telephone in advance for exact information.

The page numbers in parentheses refer to the photographs in this book.

GARDENS OPEN TO THE PUBLIC

For easy reference, the gardens mentioned in this book are listed in the same order as the chapters. A few model gardens outside France and cited in the text have also been included.

—— A Blue, White, and Green Land ——

CHÂTEAU D'HEUDICOURT
27860 Heudicourt
Tel. 32 55 86 06.   *(pp. 16, 17)*
By appointment for group visits from Easter to 1 November. Free entry every Sunday in June. These French-style gardens comprise formal parterres in the main courtyard and walks fanning out to copses. Each walk ends at a haha that opens a perspective out over the surrounding countryside. The château is open to the public.

PARC DE BEAUREPAIRE
50690 Martinvast
Tel. 33 52 02 23.   *(pp. 18, 19)*
Open all year round.
In this park situated near Cherbourg, several arrow-marked itineraries enable one to discover beautiful specimens such as tulip trees, sweet gums, bald cypresses, and exotics like araucarias and palm trees. These protect the rhododendrons, which flower in May when the park is at is best. The gardens encircle the Château de Martinvast, which is not open to the public.

—— Flower Gardens ——

CHÂTEAU DE BAILLEUL
76110 Angerville-Bailleul
Tel. 35 27 77 87.   *(pp. 64, 65)*

Open from Easter to autumn.
This park is planted with majestic beeches and oaks. Recently, the owner created an herb garden near the chapel and designed a hornbeam maze. The château is open to the public. Exhibitions of sculpted vegetation, created by artists who work with ephemeral material, are held on the grounds.

LE CLOS DU COUDRAY
76850 Etaimpuis
Tel. 35 27 77 87.   *(p. 59)*
Open from May to November.
Situated between Rouen and Dieppe, this recently created floral park is composed of plants and flowers from all over the world. More than four thousand species are grouped in theme gardens. A nursery (see p. 207) enables one to purchase plants.

FONDATION CLAUDE MONET
27620 Giverny
Tel. 32 51 28 21.   *(pp. 22, 42-45)*
Open from April to October.
Claude Monet's garden, which is laid out around his house at Giverny, is a flower and color garden. It is a *jardin de curé* where the flowerings last all through the summer months and compose a picture of stunning beauty, particularly from May to September, when the irises and the nasturtiums are in bloom. The house is open to the public.

LE JARDIN D'ANDRÉ EVE
45300 Pithiviers
Tel. 38 30 01 30.
Open from late May to late July.
In his garden, the rose specialist André Eve has assembled his favorite varieties of species, Old Garden, and modern roses. In June the garden is at its most beautiful and is deliciously perfumed.

LES JARDINS D'ANGELIQUE
Manoir de Montmain, route des Lyons
76520 Montmain
Tel. 35 79 08 12.   *(pp. 52-55)*
Open certain days in the summer months and by appointment.
Near Rouen, in front of a seventeenth-century manor house and a sheepfold, a pastel garden planted with roses and perennials.

LES JARDINS DE COTELLE
76370 Derchigny
Tel. 35 83 61 38.   *(pp. 60, 61)*
Open all year.
Throughout the passing seasons, the Cotelle family invites visitors to their garden, which features the plants which can be bought in their nursery (see p. 207).

LE MANOIR D'ARTHUR
58 rue Nationale
14220 Saint-Laurent-de-Condel
Tel. 31 79 37 81.   *(pp. 62, 63)*
Visits by appointment.
This garden near Caen is composed of perennials and shrubs disposed in mixed borders

around a Renaissance manor house. The plants were judiciously chosen to be attractive all the year round.

LE PRIEURÉ SAINT-MICHEL
61120 Croutttes
Tel. 33 39 15 15.   *(pp. 31-33)*
Open from Easter to 1 November.
Here in the Auge region, several gardens gratify the curiosity of the visitor: a rose and an iris garden, a kitchen and an herb garden, a wildflower garden, and one for aquatic plants. Every summer, exhibitions and conferences are organized on different plant themes. Accommodations (see p. 210) and boutique.

PARK AND GARDENS OF THE CHÂTEAU D'HARCOURT
14220 Thury-Harcourt
Tel. 31 79 65 41.   *(pp. 46-49)*
Open from April to October.
A park of nearly one hundred seventy-five acres surrounding the ruins of a château and bordering the river Orne. A stunning spectacle in spring and summer with flower profusion and perfection of design.

CHÂTEAU DE VANDRIMARE
27380 fleury-sur-Andelle
Tel. 32 49 03 57.   *(pp. 20, 50, 51)*
Open from May to October.
These gardens not far from the city of Rouen feature theme plantings: a hedge and flower garden, rose garden, herb garden, berry garden, and water garden. Here too are a greenhouse with tropical plants and an orangery where one can admire citrus trees in wooden boxes; the orangery can be booked for receptions.

—— Around a Château ——

CHÂTEAU DE BAILLEUL
(See above).   *(pp. 80-83)*

CHÂTEAU DE BEAUMESNIL
27140 Beaumesnil
Tel. 32 44 40 09.   *(pp. 78, 79)*
Open from May to September.
A very interesting park, notably the astonishing yew and boxwood maze planted in the moats. The château contains a bookbinding museum.

CHÂTEAU DE BIZY
27200 Vernon
Tel. 32 51 00 82.   *(pp 92-94)*
Open from April to 1 November.
This park is remarkable for its dancing waters. The water staircase, the ornamental lakes, and the fountains have now been restored. The château is open to the public.

CHÂTEAU DE BONNEVILLE
27270 Le Chamblac
Tel. 32 44 63 56.
Open from June to September by appointment.
This château, near Bernay, was formerly the residence of the writer Jean de La Varende, who restored the park and adorned it with spectacular topiaries.

CHÂTEAU DE BRÉCY
14480 Saint-Gabriel-Brécy
Tel. 31 80 11 48.   (pp. 98-101)
Open from Easter to late October.
The gardens of the Château de Brécy are situated near Bayeux. They are particularly remarkable for their terraces.

CHÂTEAU DE CANON
14270 Mézidon
Tel. 31 20 05 07.   (pp. 90, 91)
Open from Easter to September.
This park is renowned for its ornamental garden edifices and for the Chartreuses, a succession of walled gardens linked by a series of openings in archways. The château is open by appointment for group visits only.

CHÂTEAU DE CARROUGES
61320 Carrouges
Tel. 33 27 20 32.
Open all year.
The grounds of this château are adorned with very elegantly worked wrought iron gates. They are the work of Isaac Geslin who also forged those of Brécy. Le Parc Naturel Régional Normandie-Maine has its head office in the outbuildings.

CHÂTEAU DE LAUNAY
27450 Saint-Georges-du-Vièvre
Tel. 32 42 89 48.
Open all year.
Situated near the Abbaye du Bec-Hellouin, this château is surrounded by a green garden of a pure, regular design, where the clipped vegetation traces vertical and horizontal lines. A traditional, floral kitchen garden accompanies the ancient farm buildings. The château is open by appointment for group visits only.

CHÂTEAU D'O
61570 Mortrée
Tel. 33 35 33 56.
Open from April to December.
Not far from Argentan, the Château d'O is a masterpiece reflected in the water of its moats. The landscaper, Alain Richert, restored the gardens between the château and the orangery. The château is open to the public.

CHÂTEAU D'ORCHER
76700 Gonfreville-l'Orcher
Tel. 35 45 45 91.
Open all year.
The Château d'Orcher and its park are situated on the edge of a cliff which overhangs an estuary of the Seine. The greenery and the eighteenth-century design of the gardens contrast with the anarchy of the industrial universe below. A plant festival takes place at Orcher every autumn. The château is open to the public.

CHÂTEAU DE SASSY
61570 Saint-Christophe-le-Jajolet
Tel. 33 35 32 66.   (pp. 74, 95-97)
Open from spring to 1 November.
A magnificent garden à la française composed of embroidery parterres which contrast attractively with the opulent, undulating Norman landscape. The château is open to the public.

CHÂTEAU DE VENDEUVRE
14170 Saint-Pierre-sur-Dives
Tel. 31 40 93 83.   (p. 77)
Open from Easter to 1 November.
The Vendeuvre grounds are adorned with water scenes and ornamental garden follies. The château houses the Musée international du Mobilier miniature. A tea room is open to visitors.

CHÂTEAU DE VILLERS
61550 Villers-en-Ouche
Tel. 33 34 90 30.
Open in the summer and by appointment.
Situated near L'Aigle, this château (open to the public) was designed in the seventeenth century by Mansart. The park harbors garden follies.

LE HARAS DU PIN
61310 Le Pin-au-Haras
Tel. 33 39 92 01.
Open all year.
The outbuildings and the stables facing the château trace a horseshoe pattern in the axis of the garden. Many equestrian events are organized throughout the year.

—————— English Style ——————

LE BOIS DES MOUTIERS
76119 Varengeville-sur-Mer
Tel. 35 85 10 02.   (pp. 102, 105-115)
Open from March to November.
These gardens, surmounted by a large house built by Sir Edwin Lutyens, were planted by Guillaume Mallet, who followed the advice of the English landscaper Gertrude Jekyll. Rhododendrons, camellia groves, azaleas, blue hydrangeas, sequoia, and blue cedars are the glory of Le Bois des Moutiers. (The house can be visited by appointment).

LA BERQUERIE
76119 Varengeville-sur-Mer (pp. 104, 116-121)
This garden belongs to the English landscaper Mark Brown. Open by appointment only for plant lovers.

LE HARAS DE VARAVILLE
14390 Cabourg
Tel. 31 91 25 05.   (pp. 122-125)
By appointment.
This garden was designed in 1966 by the celebrated English landscaper Russell Page, according to a very structured plan. Green garden rooms, yew hedges, and banks link the eighteenth-century stables near the resolutely contemporary house. The stud farm can also be visited.

—————— Water Gardens ——————

CHÂTEAU DE NACQUEVILLE
50460 Urville-Nacqueville
Tel. 33 03 56 03.   (p. 128-133)
Open from Easter to September.
This romantic park is situated at the tip of the Cotentin. Water is omnipresent and admirably set off by extensive, natural plantings of rhododendrons, azaleas, hydrangeas, and giant gunneras.

CHÂTEAU DE SAINT-JUST
27950 Saint-Just
Tel. 32 52 21 52.   (pp. 145-147)
Open in June and July and by appointment for groups.
This park, situated near Vernon, is remarkable for its garden follies and its water scenes.

FONDATION CLAUDE MONET
27620 Giverny
Tel. 32 51 28 21.   (pp. 126, 140-144)
Open from April to October.
The water garden created by Claude Monet is separated from the flower garden by a road. It is planted with water lilies, from which the painter drew inspiration until his death.

PLANTBESSIN
14190 Castillon
Tel. 31 92 56 03.   (pp. 134-137)
Open all year.
This site, near Bayeux, sets the scene for several gardens: a water garden, a Japanese garden, an herb garden, a heather garden, and a mixed border garden. (See under Nurseries).

—————— Gourmet Gardens ——————

CHÂTEAU DE BOSMELET
76720 Auffay
Tel. 35 32 81 07.
Open by appointment.
These gardens are situated between Rouen and Dieppe. The French-style design incorporates a vast walled kitchen garden which has been given a fashionable touch with a rainbow theme.

CHÂTEAU DE GALLEVILLE
76560 Doudeville
Tel. 35 96 52 40.   (pp. 150, 158-161)
Open in July and August or by appointment for group visits.
The regular layout of the Galleville gardens, near Saint-Velay-en-Caux, was redesigned by Achille Duchêne at the beginning of the century. A walled kitchen garden combines flowers, fruit, and vegetables.

CHÂTEAU DE MIROMESNIL
Tourville-sur-Arques
76550 Offranville
Tel. 35 04 40 30.   (pp. 151-157)
Open from May to October.
Miromesnil is renowned for its kitchen garden, its vegetables, its herbaceous borders, its delphinium flowerbed, and its clematis collection. The château is open to the public.

MONT-SAINT-MICHEL
50116 Le Mont-Saint-Michel
Tel. 33 60 14 14.   (p. 171)
Open all year.
Two gardens are now open to the public: the Cloister Garden, which is enclosed by the abbey and was restored in the 1960s, and the Garden of the Large Well. An additional former plot is slated for replanting.

—————— Collectors' Gardens ——————

ARBORETUM DE L'ETOILE D'ANDAINE
61700 Champsecret
Tel. 33 37 23 17.

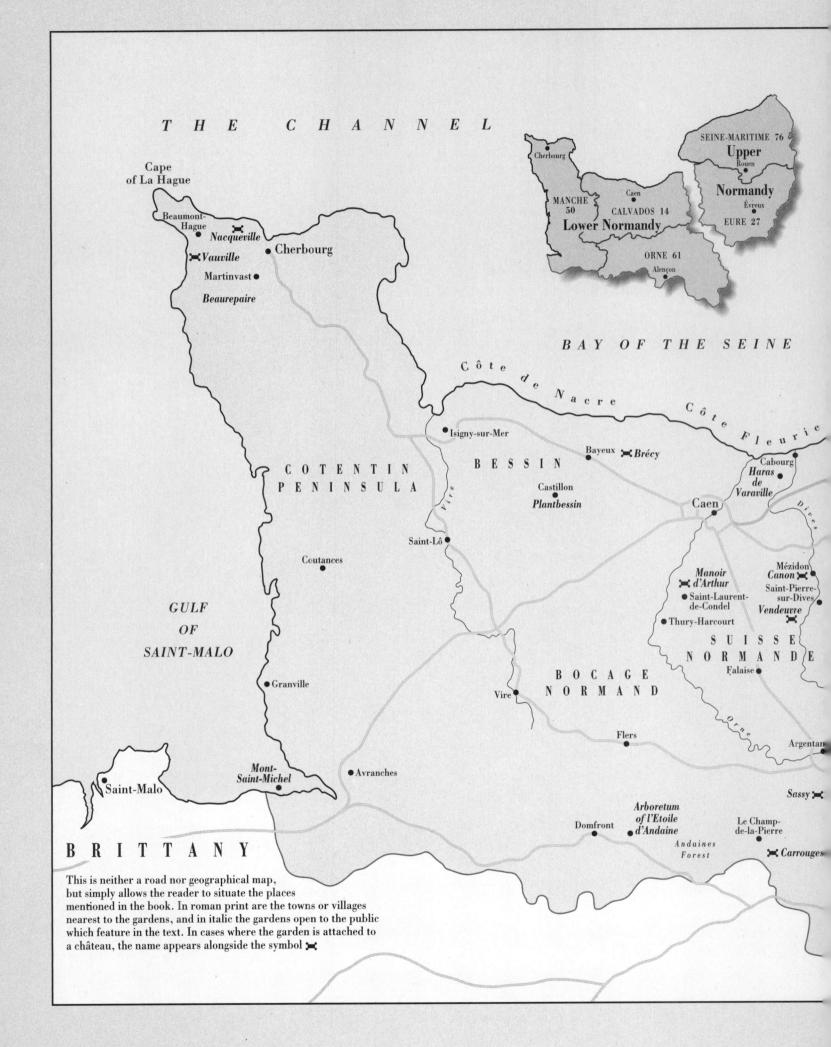

T H E   C H A N N E L

Cape
of La Hague

Beaumont-
Hague
✕ *Nacqueville*
✕ *Vauville*   ● Cherbourg
Martinvast ●
Beaurepaire

C O T E N T I N
P E N I N S U L A

GULF
OF
SAINT-MALO

● Coutances

● Granville

● Saint-Malo

Mont-
Saint-Michel

● Avranches

B R I T T A N Y

This is neither a road nor geographical map,
but simply allows the reader to situate the places
mentioned in the book. In roman print are the towns or villages
nearest to the gardens, and in italic the gardens open to the public
which feature in the text. In cases where the garden is attached to
a château, the name appears alongside the symbol ✕

SEINE-MARITIME 76
Upper
Rouen ●
Normandy

Cherbourg ●
Caen ●
Évreux ●
MANCHE
50
CALVADOS 14
Lower Normandy
EURE 27
ORNE 61
Alençon ●

B A Y   O F   T H E   S E I N E

Côte de Nacre

Côte Fleurie

● Isigny-sur-Mer

Bayeux ✕ *Brécy*   Cabourg ●
B E S S I N   *Haras*
de
Varaville

Castillon ●
Plantbessin

Caen ●

● Saint-Lô

Mézidon
Canon ✕
Saint-Pierre-
sur-Dives
Vendeuvre ✕

Manoir ✕
d'Arthur
● Saint-Laurent-
de-Condel

● Thury-Harcourt

S U I S S E
N O R M A N D E

● Falaise

B O C A G E
N O R M A N D
Vire ●

● Flers

● Argentan

Dives

Orne

Sassy ●

Arboretum
of l'Etoile
d'Andaine
Domfront ●
Andaines
Forest

Le Champ-
de-la-Pierre ●

✕ *Carrouges*

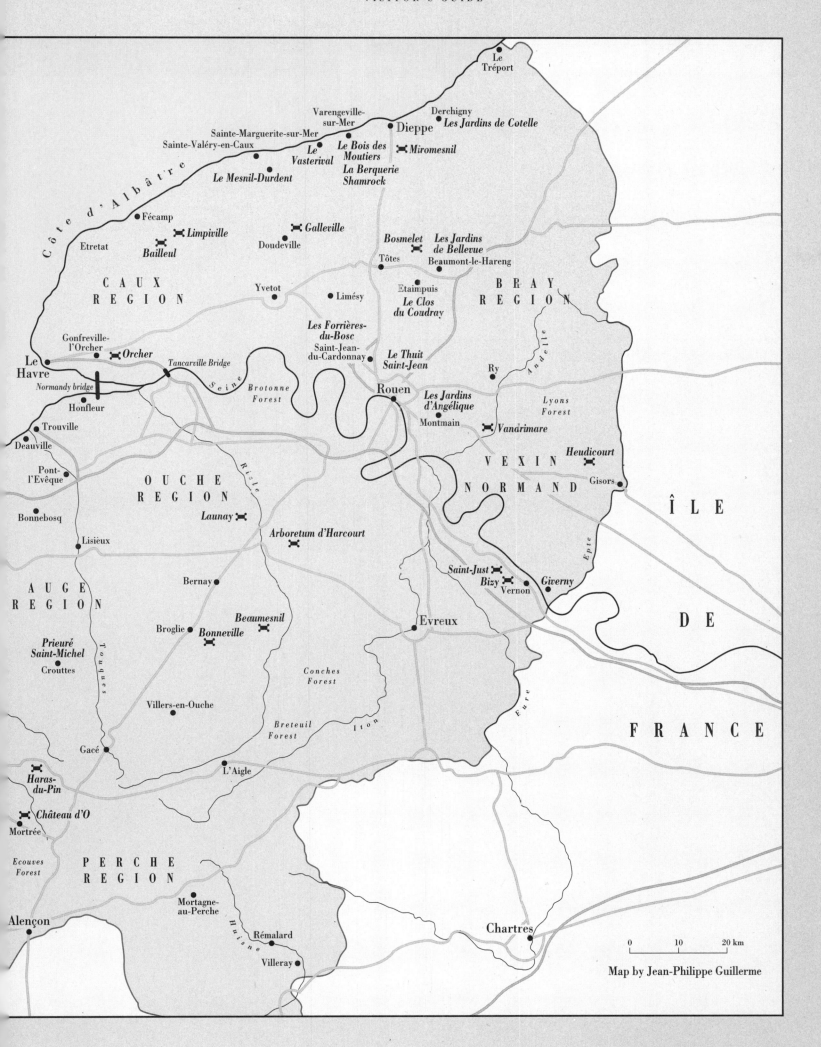

Le Tréport

Varengeville-sur-Mer

Derchigny

Les Jardins de Cotelle

Sainte-Marguerite-sur-Mer

Dieppe

Sainte-Valéry-en-Caux

Le Vasterival

Le Bois des Moutiers

Miromesnil

Le Mesnil-Durdent

La Berquerie Shamrock

Côte d'Albâtre

Fécamp

Limpiville

Galleville

Etretat

Bailleul

Doudeville

Bosmelet

Les Jardins de Bellevue

Tôtes

Beaumont-le-Hareng

CAUX REGION

Yvetot

Limésy

Etaimpuis

BRAY REGION

Le Clos du Coudray

Les Forrières-du-Bosc

Saint-Jean-du-Cardonnay

Le Thuit Saint-Jean

Ry

Andelle

Gonfreville-l'Orcher

Orcher

Tancarville Bridge

Seine

Brotonne Forest

Rouen

Lyons Forest

Le Havre

Normandy bridge

Honfleur

Les Jardins d'Angélique

Montmain

Vanarimare

Trouville

Risle

VEXIN

Heudicourt

Deauville

OUCHE REGION

NORMAND

Gisors

Pont-l'Evêque

Launay

Bonnebosq

Arboretum d'Harcourt

Epte

ÎLE

Lisieux

Saint-Just

AUGE REGION

Bernay

Bizy

Giverny

Vernon

DE

Beaumesnil

Broglie

Bonneville

Evreux

Prieuré Saint-Michel

Touques

Conches Forest

Crouttes

Eure

FRANCE

Villers-en-Ouche

Iton

Breteuil Forest

Gacé

L'Aigle

Haras-du-Pin

Château d'O

Mortrée

Ecouves Forest

PERCHE REGION

Mortagne-au-Perche

Alençon

Huisne

Rémalard

Chartres

Villeray

0   10   20 km

Map by Jean-Philippe Guillerme

Open all year.
This arboretum, situated near Domfront, was created after World War II. It covers some seventy-five acres and contains coniferous and deciduous collections.

DOMAINE D'HARCOURT
27800 Harcourt
Tel. 32 46 29 70.
Open from March to November.
This domain, situated between Evreux and Lisieux, is renowned for its arboretum, one of the largest in France, and where one finds many remarkable trees. Notable are several rare maple, beech, and oak varieties. The château, where temporary exhibitions are held, is open to the public.

LES FORRIÈRES DU BOSC
Route de Duclair
76150 Saint-Jean-du-Cardonnay
Tel. 35 33 47 06.   *(p. 184-189)*
Open from May to October.
This garden, situated near Rouen, offers an amazing collection of perennial geraniums. Geraniums can be purchased here. Botanical visits with commentary by appointment.

LES JARDINS DE BELLEVUE
76850 Beaumont-le-Hareng
Tel. 35 33 31 37.   *(pp. 175, 180-183)*
Open all year.
These gardens near Tôtes are very interesting and especially so when the hellebores and the meconopsis are in bloom (January, February, and late May). Plants can be purchased (see p. 207).

LE JARDIN DES PLANTES DE CAEN
5, place Blot
14000 Caen
Tel. 31 86 28 80.
Open all year.
These botanical gardens preserve Norman plants; harbor collections of medicinal, aromatic, and plants used in the dyeing and textile industries; and present perennial, annual, and rock garden plants.

LE JARDIN DES PLANTES DE ROUEN
114 ter, avenue des Martyrs-de-la-Résistance
76100 Rouen
Tel. 35 72 36 36.
Open all year.
This botanical establishment is to be found in a landscape garden harboring magnificent greenhouses with amazing collections of cactus, orchids, bromeliaceae, and nymphaeaceae; and several gardens offering collections of roses, irises, medicinal, and rock plants. This establishment also preserves endemic Norman plants.

LE MESNIL-DURDENT
Rue des Fougères
76450 Le Mesnil-Durdent
Tel. 35 57 14 20.
The garden can be visited all year round.
In this very small, charming village, the mayor had the idea of creating a botanical garden planted exclusively with wild plants from the Caux region. It is called Le Jardin des Amouhoques. Even the wayside plants in

the village are carefully labeled. In the town hall, interesting documentation on the plants is available.

SHAMROCK
Route de l'Eglise
76119 Varengeville-sur-Mer *(pp. 1, 172, 192, 193)*
By appointment.
Madame Corinne Mallet has gathered an amazing collection of hydrangeas here. They look lovely right from early spring, but more especially so in the summer and autumn when they take on fabulous colors.

LE THUIT SAINT-JEAN
11, Résidence du Cardonnay
76150 Saint-Jean-du-Cardonnay
Tel. 35 33 83 57.   *(p. 190, 191)*
Open from May to September by appointment.
This collection of hydrangeas near Rouen is combined with shrubs and perennial plants.

LE VASTERIVAL
76119 Sainte-Marguerite-sur-Mer
Tel. 35 85 12 05.   *(p. 174, 176-179)*
Visits by appointment only.
This celebrated garden, one of the most spectacular in the area, is of aesthetic and botanical interest. It covers some twenty acres and was created almost thirty years ago. It is a model garden that has inspired a multitude of aficionados.

VAUVILLE
Château de Vauville
50440 Beaumont-Hague
Tel. 33 52 71 41.   *(pp. 194-199)*
Open from May to October.
This botanical garden is situated at the tip of the Cotentin. It offers a collection of Mediterranean and subtropical plants. The décor is beautiful all the year round.

——— **Other Garden Attractions** ———
in France

These gardens are also worth visiting, some for their botanical interest, others for the wealth of history that is revealed at every turn.

MUSÉE AMÉRICAIN
99, rue Claude-Monet
27620 Giverny
Tel. 32 51 94 65.
Open from April to October.
It is in this historic village that the American Impressionist painters found inspiration. As a tribute, their works have been assembled in this museum. A garden designed by the landscaper Mark Rudkin is to be found in front of the building.

MUSÉE HÔTEL BAUDY
81, rue Claude-Monet
27620 Gasny
Tel. 32 21 10 03.
Open during the summer months.
In Monet's day this hotel was a rendezvous for painters. Renoir, Sisley, and Pissarro frequented it, as well as American painters such as Sargent, Robinson, and Watson. The hotel

has recently been restored. It has been transformed into a museum. The garden, whose old-fashioned style has been maintained, has been replanted with English and Old Garden roses.

JARDIN CHRISTIAN DIOR
Villa Les Rhumbs
50400 Granville
Tel. 33 61 48 21.
Open all year.
In Christian Dior's time, this garden perched on the Granville cliffs comprised a rose garden, a pergola, and a winter garden. Subsequently its beauty declined. Today efforts are being made to bring it back to life, inspired by postcards dating from its heyday.

——— **Gardens Outside France** ———

These gardens are cited in the text. Some proved to be an invaluable source of information for the creators of Norman gardens.

CHÂTEAU DE BELŒIL
7970 Belœil, Belgium
Tel. (069) 68 96 55.
This majestic property comprises copses, ornamental lakes, temples, and hornbeam bowers that are masterpieces of pruning and elegance.

EAST LAMBROOK MANOR
South Petherton, Somerset, U.K.
Tel. (0460) 40 328.
Open from March to October.
This garden, created by the celebrated Margery Fish (plant lover and author of garden books), currently offers a remarkable collection of perennial geraniums.

GREAT COMP
Platt, Borough Green, Sevenoaks, Kent, U.K.
Tel. (0732) 882 669.
Open from April to October.
This garden contains sought-after plants: heathers, roses, herbaceous borders.

INVEREWE GARDEN
Poolewe Ross and Cromarty, Highlands, U.K.
Tel. (044) 586 200.
Open all year.
This amazing Scotch garden is situated on the banks of a loch. It contains spectacular plants originating from Australia, China, New Zealand, and America, which are frost-tender but survive these latitudes due to the mildness of the climate.

KNIGHTSHAYES
Bolham, Tiverton, Devon, U.K.
Tel. (0834) 254 665.
Open from April to October.
This imposing garden is composed of a formal section around the castle and a wild garden which harbors magnolias, rhododendrons, dogwood, and wonderful tree peonies. The flowerbeds are carpeted with bulbs in the spring.

MOTTISFONT ABBEY GARDEN
Mottisfont, near Romsey, Hampshire, U.K.
Tel. (0794) 340 757.
Open from April to October.
This rose garden was created by an eminent

specialist in this field: Graham Stuart Thomas. It is pure bliss. The roses are combined with perennials chosen with great taste. This is the best place to learn about Old Garden roses.

ROYAL BOTANIC GARDEN
Edinburgh, U.K.
Tel. (031) 552 71 71.
Open all year.
This collector's garden is exceptionally abundant. Rhododendrons, magnolias, heathers, and Himalayan plants are particularly well represented. Here one can admire the largest mixed border in the United Kingdom.

SISSINGHURST GARDEN
Sissinghurst, near Cranbrook, Kent, U.K.
Tel. (0580) 712 850.
Open from April to October.
This garden of worldwide reputation is a masterpiece. It is one of the rare gardens that has maintained the spirit in which it was created, despite the fact that Vita Sackville-West and her husband Harold Nicolson are no longer with us.

SHEFFIELD PARK GARDEN
Near Uckfield, Sussex, U.K.
Tel. (0825) 790 655.
Open from April to November.
This arboretum sets the scene for trees and shrubs originating from North America and China. It is very beautiful in autumn.

TRESCO ABBEY
Tresco, Scilly Islands, U.K.
Tel. (0720) 22 349.
Open all year.
This amazing garden contains plant collections originating from South Africa, Madeira, and New Zealand. They survive here due to the Gulf Stream.

WAKEHURST PLACE GARDEN
Ardingly, near Haywards Heath,
West Sussex, U.K.
Tel. (0444) 892 701.
Open all year.
Renowned for its arboretum, but its walled garden should not be missed either. Wakehurst is associated with Kew Gardens.

NURSERIES

The plant nurseries listed below are mainly situated in Normandy. Some of those found abroad were recommended to us by garden owners. Many nurseries exhibit at the Courson, Saint-Jean-de-Beauregard, and Saint-Cloud plant fairs.

LE CLOS DU COUDRAY
76850 Etaimpuis
Tel. 35 34 96 85.
This nursery situated between Rouen and Dieppe, adjoining a floral park, possesses countless varieties of rare plants including meconopsis, primulas, and delphiniums.

CÔTÉ-JARDIN
444, route de Morgny
76160 La-Vieux-Rue
Tel. 35 34 08 87.

This nursery, near Rouen, offers an interesting selection of sought-after plants: perennials, gramineae, and perennial geraniums. They also propose designs for flowerbeds and gardens. One can draw inspiration from the adjoining garden. Mail orders can be made through their catalogue.

ELLÉBORE
La Chamotière
61360 Saint-Jouin-de-Blavou
Tel. 33 83 37 72.
In the Perche region, the nursery run by Nadine Albouy and Christian Geoffroy, two expert botanists with a passion for rare plants, specializes in hellebores, clematis, species bulbs, winter-flowering shrubs, and species peonies and irises. It is possible to make mail orders by catalogue.

ETABLISSEMENTS HORTICOLES DU COUDRY
76850 Beaumont-le-Hareng
Tel. 35 33 31 37.
Martine Lemonnier is the great specialist on hellebores, meconopsis, primulas, and perennial geraniums. Her plant nursery situated between Rouen and Dieppe offers a wide selection of these plants; one can also purchase large clumps in containers. She also sells species peonies and all kinds of shrubs. One can order these plants from the catalogue and visit the Jardin de Bellevue.

LES JARDINS DE COTELLE
76370 Derchigny
Tel. 35 83 61 38.
Near Dieppe on the D 925 road.
Frédéric and Catherine Cotelle offer a very wide range of perennial plants and shrubs. These can also be obtained by mail order from a catalogue containing a wealth of climbers, roses, heathers, ferns, perennials, bamboo, gramineae, and aromatic herbs. The owners have even designed a small aromatic herb garden for which they propose the plan and the plants (17 or 49 depending on the size). They organize theme weekends—for example, a weekend of autumn plantings.

JARDINS-PASSION
3723, route de Neufchâtel
76230 Bois-Guillaume
Tel. 35 59 19 40.
A nursery garden near Rouen specializing in topiary art, English and Old Garden roses, perennial plants for collectors, and shrubs. One can also find garden furniture and pottery.

ORKIDÉE
9, rue Grande
27220 Saint-Laurent-des-Bois
Tel. 32 37 25 22.
Here one can find collection plants chosen from perennial plants and shrubs, notably a wide choice of geraniums, hebes, and tree mallows (lavatera).

LES PÉPINIÈRES DU BOCAGE NORMAND
14410 Vassy
Tel. 31 68 53 60.
Between Uré and Condé-sur-Noireau, a nursery specializing in landscape hedging, ornamental, and apple trees.

PÉPINIÈRES DE LA CHESNAYE
14420 Ussy
Tel. 31 90 84 77.
This nursery south of Caen, near Thury-Harcourt, specializes in ornamental plants and shrubs, some of which are collector's items. A good choice of windbreak plants.

LES PÉPINIÈRES DU CLOS NORMAND
Route d'Avranches
50600 Saint-Hilaire-du-Harcou't
Tel. 33 49 10 90.
Les Pépinières du Clos Normand near Le Mont-Saint-Michel, offer a good selection of pear, cider, and eating-apple trees in fan-shaped, double, or single U espaliers. This nursery also sells ornamental trees. A mail order catalogue is available.

PÉPINIÈRES DE PLANTBESSIN
Castillon
14490 Balleroy
Tel. 31 92 56 03.
This nursery, near Bayeux, offers several rich collections of rare plants: artemisia, asters, campanulas, euphorbia, geraniums, primulas, sages, large quantities of gramineae, ferns, and aquatic plants. A catalogue is available for mail ordering.

ROSERAIE DE BERTY
07110 Largentière
Tel. 75 88 30 56.
This nursery, which is situated in the Ardèche department, supplies the plants for the kitchen garden at the Château de Villeray (see p. 168). The catalogue is as attractive as the rose garden, which contains a large quantity of Old Garden roses.

THOMSON AND MORGAN
La Melletière
61150 Saint-Ouen-sur-Maire
Tel. 33 35 85 00.
This producer of English seeds, not far from Argentan, is known all over the world for the amazing selection of plants he offers. The illustrated catalogue makes the mind boggle.

——— English Nurseries ———

BRESSINGHAM GARDENS
Bressingham, Diss, Norfolk, U.K.
Tel. (0379) 88 464.
The Bloom family is expert about perennial plants. Their nursery and catalogue offer an incomparable choice of unusual varieties, notably gramineae, ferns, Alpine plants, shrubs, climbers, conifers, and heathers.

BROADLEIGH GARDENS
Bishops Hull, Taunton, Somerset, U.K.
Tel. (0823) 286 231.
Lady Skelmersdale (who gave an enthralling conference at Courson) possesses an interesting collection of bulbs (species and hybrid varieties) which can be obtained by mail order.

DAVID AUSTIN
Bowling Green Lane, Albrighton
Wolverhampton, U.K.
Tel. (090) 722 39 31.
David Austin is the great rose "fashion designer."

He created the variety known as English roses. His nursery adjoins a rose garden that displays the varieties he has obtained. All of these roses can be purchased by mail order.

HILLIER NURSERIES
Ampfield House
Ampfield, Romsey, Hants, U.K.
Tel. (0794) 687 33.
The Hillier nursery reputation goes beyond the limits of the United Kingdom—their manual is the worldwide gardener's bible. These nurseries offer an unbelievable selection of plants of excellent quality, especially trees and shrubs. They can be obtained by mail order.

HYDON NURSERIES
Clock Barn Lane
Hydon Heath, Surrey, U.K.
Tel. (0483) 860 252.
This nursery specializes in rhododendrons. They can be obtained by mail order from the catalogue. The choice is vast. If one is looking for a very rare variety, this is the place where one has the best chance of finding it.

GARDEN DESIGN AND MAINTENANCE

Below are the contemporary landscapers mentioned in this book, as well as firms specializing in garden design and maintenance.

LOUIS BENECH
54, boulevard de La-Tour-Maubourg
75007 Paris
Tel. 44 18 04 43.
An expert botanist who has mastered the art of combining plantings with well-designed architecture. He has created mainly private gardens in France and abroad. In Paris he designed the Jardin Thomire near the Charlety stadium, and with Pascal Cribier, is currently restoring Le Jardin des Tuileries.

MARK BROWN
La Berquerie
76119 Varengeville-sur-Mer
Mark Brown is an English landscape gardener who has designed gardens in England and Normandy. He has just restored the garden of the American Impressionist painter Lilla Cabot-Perry at Giverny, which will soon be open to the public.

GILLES CLÉMENT
Acanthe
213, rue du Faubourg-Saint-Antoine
75011 Paris
Tel. 43 48 61 33.
Gilles Clément creates private and public gardens, and restores historic gardens in France and abroad. He designed the park of L'Abbaye de Valloires in the north of France, the gardens of the Château de Blois, a rose garden in Bali, and was co-creater of Le Parc Citroën in Paris.

DENIS COMONT
Agence Arc-en-Terre
30, place Alfred-de-Musset
76000 Rouen
Tel. 35 59 78 83.

He rehabilitates public gardens, sometimes works on parks such as Saint-Just, and more rarely consults on private gardens. He is the creator of the aquatic garden in Broglie, south of Bernay.

SAMUEL CRAQUELIN
Abbaye du Valasse
76210 Gruchet-le-Valasse
Tel. 35 38 00 78.
This Norman landscaper is responsible for the rehabilitation of the park in the Vallée du Telhuit in Notre-Dame-de-Gravenchon and the Jardin Japonais at the port of Le Havre, which was undertaken to commemorate its twinning with the port of Osaka. He also rehabilitates waterside sites.

PASCAL CRIBIER
6, place Edmond-Rostand
75006 Paris
Tel. 43 26 46 46.
He takes over and revives sites with his innovations, whether they be public or private gardens. Among his official commissions, one might mention the Opéra Bastille, where he installed patios (which unfortunately are out-of-sight to the public) and the park of Le Fort d'Aubervilliers. He is currently working with Louis Benech on the restoration of Le Jardin des Tuileries.

CLOTILDE DUVOUX-BOUCHAYER
14, rue Rémilly
78000 Versailles
Tel. 39 50 44 58.
Clotilde Duvoux-Bouchayer rehabilitates old parks and works for l'Association régionale des Parcs et Jardins de Haute-Normandie. She is currently restoring the plant heritage of the Manoir de Villers, where she is designing small ornamental gardens.

ARABELLA LENNOX-BOYD
45 Moreton Street
London, U.K.
Tel. (071) 931 99 95.
Highly reputed in England (several gold medals at the Chelsea Flower Show), she has worked in France, Spain, and in Belgium, where she transformed the park of the royal residence, Château du Belvédère.

GUILLAUME PELLERIN
9 *bis*, rue d'Assas
75006 Paris
Tel. 42 22 90 03.
This architect also designs gardens. The first one he created was that of his friend and neighbor, the author Jacques Prévert, in the Cotentin.

ALAIN RICHERT
Le Moulin de Vau
61570 Boucé
Alain Richert teaches garden art at l'Ecole nationale supérieure du Paysage de Versailles. Among other things, he is the creator of Le Labyrinthe aux Oiseaux d'Yvoire, of a medieval and Renaissance garden in the Deux-Sèvres department, and of a sixteenth-century style orchard-arboretum in Ballon in the Sarthe department.

Specialized firms

BESNEUX
12, avenue Charles-de-Gaulle
14390 Cabourg
Tel. 31 91 01 56.
This firm creates, transforms, maintains, and restores parks and private gardens in Normandy and in the Ile-de-France.

WEEK-END SERVICE
Chemin de Gassart
14130 Saint-Hymer
Tel. 31 64 10 58.
This firm, situated near Pont-l'Evêque, lays out and maintains parks and gardens. They execute sophisticated large-scale works in collaboration with landscapers like Franz Baechler or Louis Benech.

GARDEN DECOR

BESNEUX
12, avenue Charles-de-Gaulle
14390 Cabourg
Tel. 31 91 01 56.
This garden maintenance firm (see above) also sells furniture, pottery, pergolas, etc.

CHRISTIAN PLACHOT
76240 Belbeuf
Saint-Adrien
Tel. 35 02 00 40.
Quite near Rouen, Christian Plachot proposes traditional materials as well as ornamental garden antiques: wrought iron chairs and tables, cast iron Medici vases, stone vases, statues, and pottery.

JARDINS IMAGINAIRES
9 *bis*, rue d'Assas
75006 Paris
Tel. 42 22 90 03.
Cléophée de Turckheim and Guillaume Pellerin, owners of the Château de Vauville, keep a boutique in Paris where they propose some new, but mainly antique, objects to decorate a garden: fountains, tools, and all kinds of charming items.

JARDINS-PASSION
3723, route de Neufchâtel
76230 Bois-Guillaume
Tel. 35 59 19 40.
In their boutique near Rouen, Patrick Amiet and Thierry Clavier propose everything that touches gardens: books, plants, advice, and objects for decorating a garden: teak furniture, hanging baskets, and beautiful English tools.

SEMA
Carrefour de Malbrouck, RN 13
27300 Carsix
Tel. 32 44 96 20.
Here, not far from Bernay, one can find architectural elements and antique ornaments to animate and decorate a garden: marble fountains, wrought iron gates, stone basins, statues, troughs, and benches.

VOLUBILIS
36, route de Paris
27380 Bourg-Beaudouin
Tel. 32 49 36 00.

This is a second-hand garden store.
Everything here is antique: floral crockery, old garden books, vases, lamps, arbors, summer-houses, pergolas, statues, bell-jars, wickerwork.

PLANT FESTIVALS

Plant fairs enable one to acquire plants, to find out about the latest hybrids, and to keep up on garden news in general.

CHELSEA FLOWER SHOW
Inquiries to the Royal Horticultural Society
80, Vincent Square
London, U.K.
Tel. (071) 834 43 33.
This floral event of worldwide reputation takes place in London in May and lasts one week. Under the large white tent, flowers at the peak of their beauty are displayed. Outside, one can draw inspiration from small gardens created by celebrated landscapers.

FÊTES DES PLANTES, DE L'ARBRE ET DE LA FORÊT
Château de Mesnières-en-Bray
76270 Neufchâtel-en-Bray
Tel. 35 93 10 14.
This plant festival usually takes place in May. One can buy trees, shrubs, perennial, and annual plants, bulbs, and Old Garden roses.

FÊTES DES PLANTES DU CHÂTEAU DE VENDEUVRE
14170 Saint-Pierre-sur-Dives
Tel. 31 400 93 83.
For many years, nurseries and other exhibitors from the region have formed a magnificent gathering the last weekend in April. It is one of the most important horticultural events in Normandy. Organized this year by the dynamic association Art et Jardins de Normandie.

FOIRE AUX ARBRES ET AUX PLANTES DE LISIEUX
BP 222
14107 Lisieux Cedex
Tel. 31 31 16 10.
Formerly called La Foire aux Pépins, that is to say the fruit-tree fair, this event proposes shrubs and ornamental trees.

FOIRE AUX GÉRANIUMS
14430 Beuvron-en-Auge
Tel. 31 79 23 31.
Quite near Caen, this geranium, or to be more precise, pelargonium fair is a tradition. It was created in this charming village to encourage the inhabitants to decorate their houses with flowers. At the beginning of May the best producers exhibit pelargoniums, petunias, and surfinia. The fair now proposes perennials.

PLANTES EN FÊTE AU CHÂTEAU D'ORCHER
Château d'Orcher
76700 Gonfreville-l'Orcher
Tel. 35 45 45 91.
During the second weekend of October, one should go to the Château d'Orcher, near Le Havre, to acquire plants or garden furniture, garden books, listen to conferences, and attend floral demonstrations. This is the rendezvous

of eminent specialists and renowned garden photographers, who exhibit their work.

EN ROUTE TO THE GARDENS OF NORMANDY

A few itineraries are listed below to help the reader discover the landscape and visit the gardens in Normandy. Brochures for these circuits can be had from the Comité Régionale de Tourisme de Normandie, Le Doyenné, 14, rue Charles-Corbeau, 27000 Evreux (Tel. 32 33 79 00).

CIRCUIT DE LA DAME AUX CAMÉLIAS
Office de Tourisme
Mairie de Gacé
61230 Gacé
Tel. 33 35 50 24.
The heroine of this work by Dumas was based on a real person, Alphonsine Plessis. This itinerary around Gacé retraces her travels in Normandy.

CIRCUIT MONET
Château d'Auvers
Rue de Léry
95430 Auvers-sur-Oise
Tel. 34 48 48 50.
The Château d'Auvers organizes circuits that link such meccas of Impressionism as Auvers and Giverny. The trip to Monet's house and garden is undertaken by bus and boat, and lunch is served on the lake.

EQUI'DAYS
Comité départemental du tourisme du Calvados
Place du Canada
14000 Caen
Tel. 31 86 53 30.
In October, when all the apple trees are bearing fruit, the Calvados department pays tribute to its horses by organizing Equi'days. This is when the stud farms and horse breeders organize open days for the public, a time to admire the horses and the architecture of the old manor houses often tucked away in a delightful green countryside.

ROUTE HISTORIQUE DES DUCS DE NORMANDIE
Château de Vandeuvre
14170 Saint-Pierre-sur-Dives
Tel. 31 40 93 83.
This itinerary across the Auge region and the Suisse Normande leads to châteaux, manor houses, abbeys, gardens, and sites of historical and architectural interest, such as Le Prieuré Saint-Michel, the park of the château de Canon, and that of the château d'Harcourt.

ROUTE HISTORIQUE DES MAISONS D'ECRIVAINS
13, avenue d'Eylau
75116 Paris
Tel. 47 27 45 51.
This circuit between Paris and Rouen enables one to discover Casimir Delavigne's houses near Tourny, Michelet's château in Vascoeuil, Flaubert's house in Croisset, Jean de La Varende's château in Bonneville (see p. 88) and Victor Hugo's house in Villequier.

ROUTE HISTORIQUE DES PARCS ET JARDINS DE BASSE-NORMANDIE
Le Prieuré Saint-Michel
61120 Crouttes
Tel. 33 39 15 15.
This visit to Lower Normandy enables one to discover its plant, landscape, and architectural heritage. Sassy, Canon, Thury-Harcourt, Brécy, Christian Dior's garden, the Château d'O, Vauville, Plantbessin, and Beaurepaire figure high on the list.

ROUTE HISTORIQUE DES PARCS ET JARDINS ILE-DE-FRANCE ET NORMANDIE
Maison de Chateaubriand
87, rue Chateaubriand
92290 Chatenay-Malabry
Tel. 47 02 58 61.
The circuit starts from the Ile-de-France and takes the participants to Normandy where they are offered visits of Giverny, Bizy, Harcourt, Miromesnil, as well as Le Bois des Moutiers.

ROUTE NORMANDIE-VEXIN
Château de Bizy
27200 Vernon
Tel. 32 51 00 82.
A tourist itinerary between Paris and Rouen going from châteaux to gardens, and from abbeys to museums—Gaillon, Bizy, and Giverny are included in the circuit.

ROUTE TOURISTIQUE DU PAYS SEINE-ANDELLE
Comité départemental de tourisme de l'Eure
Hôtel du Département
27003 Evreux
Tel. 32 31 51 51.
This circuit enables one to admire the very beautiful Norman dovecotes to be found in the country, in villages, or belonging to an abbey or a manor. They are often difficult to find and this itinerary is the best way to see them.

GARDEN ASSOCIATIONS

These associations can be very useful for gardening enthusiasts. They are an endless source of ideas and information and provide access to new privately opened gardens.

ART ET JARDINS DE NORMANDIE
BP 2055
14019 Caen Cedex
Tel. 31 82 66 91.
An association of amateurs and professionals. It organizes conferences, journeys abroad, and visits to private gardens otherwise inaccessible to the public.

ASSOCIATION DES AMIS DE LA COLLECTION D'HYDRANGEAS 'SHAMROCK'
Route de l'Eglise
76119 Varengeville-sur-Mer
Members of this association can expand their knowledge of the hydrangea genus and follow the evolution of the 'Shamrock' hydrangeas cultivated by Corinne Mallet.

ASSOCIATION RÉGIONALE DES PARCS ET JARDINS DE HAUTE-NORMANDIE
7, rue de Trianon
76100 Rouen
Tel. 35 72 36 36.

This association organizes exhibitions on garden art and visits to private or public gardens in Normandy and elsewhere. The association has drawn up an inventory of gardens in Upper Normandy and encourages its members to have their gardens surveyed by local landscapers.

ASSOCIATION RÉGIONALE DES PARCS ET JARDINS DE BASSE-NORMANDIE
Domaine de Beaurepaire
50690 Martinvast
Tel. 33 52 02 23.
This association has the same mandate as the one above.

ENTRE SEINE ET JARDINS
Manoir de Villers
30, route de Sahurs
76113 Saint-Pierre-de-Manneville
Tel. 35 32 07 02.
From Rouen to Villequier along the Seine valley, this association invites members to discover châteaux, manors, abbeys, villages, and orchards. It also organizes meetings with horticulturists and events with floral themes.

ESPRIT DE JARDIN
2 rue Edouard-Larue
76600 Le Havre
Tel. 35 48 75 92.
This association, of which the comtesse d'Harcourt is the honorary president, encourages the creation of sites devoted to plants and the study of horticulture through conferences and visits to private gardens.

SOCIÉTÉ CENTRALE D'HORTICULTURE DE CAEN ET DU CALVADOS
Hôtel de Ville
39, rue Desmoueux
14000 Caen
Tel. 31 85 77 07.
This society organizes trips in France to flower festivals, and organizes courses on perennial plants and fruit tree cultivation.

ACCOMODATIONS AND DINING IN GARDEN SETTINGS

As this book proposes visits to gardens and trips across Normandy, we thought it useful to offer a few suggestions for a pleasant stay in floral surroundings. One of the charms of Normandy is the large number of farmsteads and manors offering accommodation to visitors. Hereunder are some addresses, from the simplest to the most grand.

CHÂTEAU D'AUDRIEU
14250 Audrieu
Tel. 31 80 21 52.
Situated in the Calvados department, this château is surrounded by sixty acres of English-style gardens planted with three-hundred-year-old trees. A French-style garden and mixed borders serve as a showcase for the château. A kitchen garden, an herb garden, and a white

garden contribute to the charm. This hotel is listed in the Relais et Châteaux chain.

CHÂTEAU DES AYGUES
Rue Jacques-Offenbach
76790 Etretat
Tel. 35 28 92 77.
This small nineteenth-century château, where the queens of Spain liked to stay, offers guest rooms with beautiful antique furniture. Michel Lorgeoux is a charming host. He has recently had the gardens restored and gives advice on the best walks in the area.

CHÂTEAU DE BELLE-ISLE-SUR-RISLE
112, route de Rouen
27500 Pont-Audemer
Tel. 322 56 96 22.
20 km from Honfleur, on an island in the river, this grand nineteenth-century residence is surrounded by five acres planted with approximately one thousand roses and century-old trees.

CHÂTEAU DE SAINT-RÉMY
La Maroisière, Saint-Rémy-sur-Orne
14570 Clecy
Tel. 31 69 84 06.
In the heart of the Suisse Normande, this small château opens its doors to passing guests. The owner is Australian. He takes great care of his garden, which is renowned in the region and where it is very pleasant to have breakfast.

LE COTTAGE DE LA VOISINIÈRE
50410 Percy
Tel. 33 61 18 47.
Not far from Avranches, Maryclaude Duchemin offers accommodation in very simple, small houses surrounded by a cottage garden that displays flowers all the year round. The rooms are comfortable and full of charm. Breakfast can be served in the garden.

COUR L'EPÉE
14340 Saint-Aubin Lebizay
Tel. 31 65 09 45.
Near Cabourg, this small hamlet of half-timbered houses is charming. An idyllic place to stay, with a view over a traditional Norman landscape. These guest rooms are so much in demand that advance reservation is imperative.

DOMAINE DE CHAMPDIEU
76590 Gonneville-sur-Scie
Tel. 35 32 66 82.
A half-timbered farm, not far from Dieppe, in perfect harmony with the wooded landscape. It nestles in a romantic English-style garden, offers three rooms with antique furniture, and very refined evening meals.

DOMAINE DE LA PICQUOTERIE
14230 La Cambe
Tel. 31 92 09 82.
Jean-Gabriel Laloy has carefully restored an old fortified farm near Bayeux and graced it

with several gardens: one with perennial plants; a green, white, and silver garden; an herb garden; and a French-style garden. The manor welcomes guests all year round.

LA FERME DES POIRIERS ROSES
Saint-Philibert-des-Champs
14130 Pont-L'Evêque
Tel. 31 64 72 14.
A world of flowers surrounds this half-timbered seventeenth-century farm, very typical of the Auge region, which offers guests rooms (each of which is unique). Countless bouquets decorate the bedrooms and the drawing room where delicious breakfasts are served. It is advisable to reserve in advance.

FERME SAINT-SIMÉON
Rue Adolphe-Marais
14600 Honfleur
Tel. 31 89 23 61.
La Ferme Saint-Siméon, formerly a simple inn, served as the rendezvous for Boudin, Corot, Monet, and Jongkind. It was transformed into a large comfortable house, and the garden was redesigned to grow flowers, fruit, and vegetables. It is now an elegant hotel in beautiful surroundings where it is always pleasant to stay.

LE HOMME
Poilly, Le Bourg
50220 Ducey
Tel. 33 48 44 41.
Near Mont Saint-Michel, a simple but comfortable house offers rooms at reasonable prices. Hydrangeas abound in the calm flower garden.

LE MANOIR DU CHAMP VERSANT
14340 Bonnebosq
Tel. 31 65 11 07.
This charming little half-timbered manor house dates from the sixteenth century. It provides a very pleasant stopping place in the Calvados department with two guest rooms enhanced with beautiful stone fireplaces.

LE MOULIN DE CONNELLES
40, route d'Amfreville
27430 Connelles
Tel. 32 59 53 33.
This nineteenth-century Anglo-Norman manor house is situated near one of the loops of the Seine near Louviers. It is surrounded by a seven-acre landscape park and planted with beautiful tall trees. Elegant rooms and refined cooking.

LE PRIEURÉ SAINT-MICHEL
61120 Crouttes
Tel. 33 39 15 15.
This old Benedictine priory is surrounded by several gardens and notably by a rose garden (see pp. 30, 32). The guest rooms are located in one of the old buildings, and a small former bakery can accommodate four guests. Numerous activities in the summer.

CALENDAR OF FLOWERINGS

This calendar indicates the important moments throughout the passing seasons that embellish the gardens in Normandy and the ideal periods for visiting gardens open to the public.

SPRING

Magnolias: Le Bois des Moutiers and Le Vasterival
flowering cherry: Le Vasterival
Cotoneaster: the turtles at Bailleul
Rhododendrons: Beaurepaire, Le Bois des Moutiers, Nacqueville, and Le Vasterival
Subtropical plants: Vauville
Perennial geraniums: Les Forrières du Bosc
Irises: Giverny
Meconopsis: Les Jardins de Bellevue
Primulas: Les Jardins de Bellevue
All perennials: Le clos du Coudray, Les Jardins de Cotelle, Le Manoir d'Arthur, Plantbessin, Vandrimare, Le Vasterival

SUMMER

Hydrangeas: Le Thuit Saint-Jean, Shamrock, Le Vasterival
Roses: Le Bois des Moutiers, Les Jardins d'Angélique, Le Prieuré Saint-Michel, Vandrimare
flowers and vegetables: Bosmelet, Galleville, Miromesnil, Mont-Saint-Michel
Nasturtiums: Giverny
Delphiniums: Miromesnil
Perennial geraniums: Les Forrières du Bosc
Aquatic or semi-aquatic plants: Le Clos du Coudray, Giverny, Plantbessin, Vandrimare, Vendeuvre
Aromatic plants: Bailleul, Le Clos du Coudray, Vandrimare
All varieties: Le Bois des Moutiers, Canon, Le Clos du Coudray, Les Jardins de Cotelle, Le Manoir d'Arthur, Plantbessin, Thury-Harcourt, Vandrimare, Le Vasterival

AUTUMN

Beeches: Bailleul
Hydrangeas: Le Thuit Saint-Jean, Shamrock, Le Vasterival
Vegetables: Bosmelet, Galleville, Miromesnil, Mont-Saint-Michel
Asters: Giverny, Les Jardins de Cotelle, Le Manoir d'Arthur, Plantbessin
Nasturtiums: Giverny
All varieties: Le Vasterival

WINTER

Camellias: Le Vasterival
Mahonias: Le Bois des Moutiers, Le Vasterival
Hellebores: Les Jardins de Bellevue, Le Vasterival

GLOSSARY

ANNUAL: A plant that completes its life cycle in one growing season.

ARBORETUM: A botanical tree garden where trees and shrubs are cultivated for educational and scientific purposes.

AVENUE: A majestic walk or broad passageway bordered by ornamental trees, generally leading to a place of residence. Also called an allée.

BIENNIAL: A plant that flowers and dies one year after its seeds have been sown. It will produce roots, stems, and leaves during its first year and then fruit or flowers during its second year before it dies.

BOTANICAL ROSES: Roses that are found growing wild in nature. Also called wild roses.

BOTANICAL SPECIES: Wild or uncultivated plants or flowers found growing in a natural environment.

BOWLING GREEN: A smooth lawn, originally used for playing bowls. It can be open with surrounding slopes, or reinforced by borders of clipped shrubs, pruned boxtrees, or thickets,

BRODERIE: Embroidery parterres that are composed of clipped shrubs, such as boxtrees; flowers; or crushed slate or tiles and colored stones. They often form elaborate ornamental motifs that are reminiscent of needlepoint work. Characteristic of many formal gardens.

COMPOST: A mixture composed mainly of cow manure and decomposed organic matter, such as leaves, weeds, and kitchen waste, which is used to condition and fertilize the soil.

COROLLA: The part of the flower formed by the petals.

CULTIVAR: A variety of plant or flower originating and persistent under cultivation.

DOVECOTE: A small house or houselike building that is used for taming and breeding doves or pigeons.

ENGLISH GARDEN: A garden, which appeared in England during the eighteenth century, that imitates nature. Also called a landscape garden or a garden à l'anglaise.

ENGLISH ROSES: Roses that were developed during recent years by the British rose cultivator David Austin. They were created by crossing Old Garden roses with modern hybrid roses.

ESPALIER: A railing or trellis on which fruit trees or shrubs can be trained to grow flat. An espaliered tree is one that has been trained to grow flat against a wall or some other support.

FASTIGIATE: A term describing trees whose branches grow vertically in a nearly parallel position rather than spread out.

FRENCH GARDEN: A garden that is extremely regular and well-proportioned as to form, arrangement, and design, arranged around an axis dominated generally by a château, which includes perspectives, embroidery parterres, hedgerows, or clipped shrubs. Also called a formal garden or a garden à la française.

FROST-TENDER: Plants that are particularly sensitive or vulnerable to frost.

GENUS: A class, kind, or group marked by common characteristics or by one common characteristic. In the classification of plants, it is a major category that is more specific than the family and more general than the species.

GLACIERE: Also known as an outdoor icehouse. An underground structure or pit, with insulated walls and roof, that contains snow or blocks of ice and which is used for storage of perishables.

HA-HA: A hedge or wall constructed to surround a garden, but set low in a ditch so as not to obstruct the view and to prevent livestock from entering. Its name is said to have originated from the exclamation of surprise expressed by English strollers when they suddenly came upon one of the large ditches, which was not visible from a distance. Also called a sunk fence or a saut-de-loup.

HYBRID PERPETUAL ROSES: Any of several hardy rose bushes derived from the bourbon rose.

MIROIR D'EAU: An ornamental pond or lake, sometimes vast in size, often featured in formal gardens. Also called a reflecting pool or basin.

MIXED BORDER: A flowerbed cultivated with annual, biennial, or perennial plants, or with bulbs or shrubs.

MODERN ROSES: Roses that were created after 1900.

MULCH: A mixture of matter such as dead leaves, pine needles, and straw, or sawdust or paper, that is spread on the ground around plants and trees to form a protective covering which helps to reduce evaporation, maintain an even soil temperature, nourish the plants, prevent the growth of weeds, enrich the soil, and prevent erosion.

OLD GARDEN ROSES: Those species of roses that were created between 1800 and 1920, such as Portland, Noisette, Bourbon, and hybrids.

PANICLE: A loosely branched flower cluster, often pyramidal in shape.

PARTERRE: An ornamental garden, often divided into sections arranged to form a pattern, with paths running between the beds. It can be composed of grass, flowers, shrubs, or water.

PERENNIAL: A plant that develops and produces flowers or fruit during spring and summer, then dies off in winter, and reappears again the following spring. It will live for at least three seasons, but can survive for several years or more, following the same process of growth.

PERGOLA: An arbor or covered garden walk that is created by training vegetation or flowers to grow over latticework or rafters supported by posts. Also called a bower.

POTAGER: A garden where vegetables and certain fruits are cultivated for consumption. Often features ornamental plants. Also called a kitchen garden.

TAPIS VERT: A vast grass parterre, generally rectangular in shape or gently sloping.

TERRACED GARDEN: A garden constructed on several tiers that allows a good view of the countryside. Also known as a garden à l'italienne.

TOPIARY: The practice or art of training, cutting, and pruning plants, principally yew trees and boxtrees, into ornamental shapes that form plant sculptures.

PLANTS IN THE GARDENS OF NORMANDY

Here, classified by chapter, are the plants mentioned in this book.

FLOWER GARDENS
Trees and shrubs
Abelia
Amelanchier canadensis
Arbutus
Aronia: chokeberry
Berberis: barberry
Buxus: box
Camellia
Carpinus: hornbeam
Caryopteris
Ceanothus impressus: California lilac
Choisya ternata: Mexican orange
Cornus florida 'Cherokee Chief'
 C. nuttallii
 'Portlemouth': dogwood
Cotinus
Cotoneaster
Cryptomeria: Japanese cedar
Daphne
Eleagnus
Euonymus 'Red Cascade'
Fagus: beech
Garrya elliptica
Hamamelis mollis: witch hazel
Hibiscus
Hovenia dulcis: raisin-tree
Hydrangea 'Annabelle'
 H. 'Preziosa'
 H. 'White Wave'
Ilex: holly
Magnolia
Mahonia
Malus 'Everest': 'Everest' apple
Nandina
Nyssa sinensis: Chinese tupelo
 N. sylvatica: black gum
Parrotia pendula
Pieris
Prunus cerasifera 'Pissardii': cherry plum
Pyracantha: firethorn
Pyrus salicifolia 'Pendula': willow-leaved pear
Rhododendron
Rubus thibetanus
Senecio 'Sunshine'
Taxus: yew
Viburnum bodnantense
 V. davidii,
 V. plicatu 'Mariesii'
 V. tinus: laurustinus

Climbing plants
Actinidia kolomikta
Clematis 'General Sikorski'
 C. 'Madame Lecoultre'
 C. montana
 C. 'Perle d'Azur'
Hydrangea petiolaris
Jasminum: jasmine
Lonicera japonica: honeysuckle
Parthenocissus: Virginia creeper
Passiflora: passionflower
Tropaeolum: nasturtium
Vitis coignetiae
Wisteria

Roses
'Abraham Darby'
'Adélaïde d'Orléans'
'Albéric Barbier'
'Albertine'
'Bordure d'Or'
'Bordure de Nacre'
'Bordure Rose'
'Buff Beauty'
'Candeur'

'Centenaire de Lourdes'
'Château d'Amboise'
'Comte de Chambord'
'Dorothy Perkins'
'Fair Bianca'
'Gloire de Dijon'
'Golden Wing'
'Graham Thomas'
'Grand Nord'
'Grand Siècle'
'Héritage'
'Iceberg'
'Jacques Cartier'
'Jardin de Bagatelle'
'Leverkusen'
'Little White Pet'
'Madame Alfred Carrière'
'Madame Delbard'
'Madame Meilland'
'Mermaid'
'Milrose'
'Nevada'
'Queen Elizabeth'
'Salet'
'Tobago'
'Weichenblau'
'Winchester Cathedral'
'Zephirine Drouin'
Rosa hugonis, R. pteracantha, R. rugosa

Perennials, annuals, biennials, and bulbs
Achillea millefolium: milfoil
Agapanthus
Ageratum
Alchemilla mollis
Anaphalis
Anethum graveolens: dill
Aquilegia: columbine
Artemisia 'Powis Castle'
Asclepias tuberosa: butterfly weed
Aster 'Alma Potschke'
 A. cordifolium 'Ideal'
 A. frikartii
Astilbe
Astrantia
Avena sempervirens: oats
Campanula lactiflora
Carlina acanthifoliam
Catananche caerulea: Cupid's darts
Centaurea
Centranthus ruber 'Albus': valerian
Cephalaria gigantea
Cheiranthus: wallflower
Chrysanthemum
Cleome
Convolvulus cneorum: bindweed
Cosmos
Crocosmia
Cyclamen
Dahlia
Delphinium
Diascia
Digitalis: foxglove
Elymus arenarius
Epilobium
Erica arboria: tree heather
Eryngium
Eupatorium
Euphorbia amygdaloides
 var. *robbiae*: Mrs. Robb's bonnet
 var. *wulfenii*
 E. characias,
 E. martinii
 E. polychroma: spurges
Ferns
Fuschia

Galanthus nivalis: snowdrop
Gaura
Geranium clarkei 'Kashmir White'
 G. endressii: French crane's bill
 G. himalayense 'Johnson's Blue'
 G. macrorrhizum: Balkan crane's bill
 G. magnificum
 G. phaeum: dusky crane's bill
 G. psilostemon
 G. renardii,
 G. sylvaticum: wood crane's bill
Gunnera manicata
Helianthemum: rock rose
Helianthus: sunflower
Helichrysum: 'everlasting'
Hemerocallis: daylily
Hesperis matronalis: dame's violet
Hosta
Iris germanica,
 I. kaempferi,
 I. sibirica
Isatis tinctoria
Japanese anemone
Lavandula: lavender
Lavatera
Lilium candidum: Madonna lily
Lilium regale: royal lily
Lunaria annua: honesty
Lupinus: lupin
Lysimachia clethroides: loosestrife
Macleaya cordata: plume poppy
Malva moschata 'Alba': musk mallow
Meconopsis betonicifolia: Himalayan blue poppy
Mentha: mint
Monarda: bergamot
Montbretia
Nepeta 'Six Hills Giant': catmint
Onopordum
Origanum: oregano
Paeonia: peony
Papaver 'Perry's White'
 P. rhoeas: poppy
Penstemon
Pervoskia
Phlomis fruticosa: Jerusalem sage
Phlomis samia
Phlox
Physostegia: obedient plant
Polygonum campanulatum
Primula flaccida
Romneya coulteri: Matilija poppy
Rudbeckia
Ruta graveolens: rue
Salvia: sage
Santolina: lavender cotton
Saxifraga: saxifrage
Scabiosa caucasica
Sedum 'Autumn Joy': stonecrop
Silphium perfolatum
Solidaster
Stachys lanata: lamb's tongue
Thalictrum dipterocarpum: meadow rue
Thymus: thyme
Verbascum: mullein
Zinnia

AROUND A CHÂTEAU
Trees and shrubs
Aesculus: horse chestnut
Buxus sempervirens 'Suffruticasa'
B. sempervirens: box
Carpinus: hornbeam
Castanea sativa: chestnut
Cedrus atlantica: cedar
 C. libani: cedar of Lebanon
Fagus sylvatica: common beech

 F. sylvatica purpurea: purple beech
Malus: apple
 M. 'Everest': 'Everest' apple
Pinus sylvestris: Scotch pine
Pyrus: pear
Quercus: oak
Rhododendron
Rosa 'Blanc Double de Coubert'
 R. 'Golden Wing'
 R. 'Jacques Cartier'
Syringa: lilac
Taxus: yew
Tilia: linden
Flowers
Calendula: marigold
Clematis wilsonii
Coreopsis
Cosmos
Dahlia
Gladiolus
Helenium
Phlox
Polemonium
Solidago: goldenrod

Herbs
Allium schoenoprasum: chive
Artemisia dracunculus: tarragon
Brassica oleracea: kale
Mentha: mint
Rosmarinus officinalis: rosemary
Rumex: savory
Satureia: sorrel
Thymus: thyme

ENGLISH STYLE
Trees and shrubs
Acer: maple
Arbutus
Buddleja
Camellia
Carpinus japonicus: hornbeam
Cedrus atlantica: cedar
Cercidiphyllum: katsura
Cotinus
Deutzia
Elaeagnus
Fagus: beech
Gaultheria
Hydrangea involucrata
 H. paniculata 'Kiushu'
Ilex: holly
Magnolia grandiflora
 M. stellata 'Water Lily'
Mahonia
Paeonia: peony
Pinus sylvestris: Scotch pine
Pyrus salicifolia 'Pendula': willow-leaved pear
Quercus ilex: holm oak
Rhododendron halopeanum
 R. williamsianum
Rhodotypos
Rosmarinus: rosemary
Taxus: yew
Viburnum davidii
 V. plicatum 'Mariesii'

Perennials, annuals, biennials, and bulbs
Aconitum: monkshood
Allium christophii
Aquilegia
Artemisia arborescens
Arum
Aster divaricatus
Calendula: marigold
Carex
Centranthus ruber: valerian
Cheiranthus: wallflower
Colchicum: meadow saffron

Cornus canadensis
Crocus pulchellus
Delphinium
Dicentra spectabilis:
  Dutchman's breeches
Digitalis: foxglove
Echinacea purpurea
Eryngium
Eschscholzia: California poppy
Euphorbiae amygdaloides 'Rubra':
  wood spurge
Ferns
Foeniculum vulgare 'Bronze': fennel
Fritillaria imperialis
Geranium
Hebe
Helleborus: hellebore
Hosta
Iris kaempferi
Kniphofia 'Modesta'
Lavandula: lavender
Lilium candidum: Madonna lily
Lupinus: lupin
Macleaya cordata: plume poppy
Malva moschata 'Alba':
  musk mallow
Miscanthus sinensis 'Gracillimus'
  M. sinensis 'Silver Feather'
Nepeta: catmint
Petasites japonicus var. *giganteus*:
  giant butterburr
Phlox
Plantago major 'Atropurpureum':
  plantain
Polemonium nipponicum
  'Album'
Polygonum copanulatum
Pulmonaria rubra 'Sissinghurst
  White': lungwort
Ranunculus acris: bachelor's button
Rodgersia
Rosmarinus: rosemary
Ruta graveolens: rue
Salvia nemerosa: sage
Santolina neapolitana:
  lavender cotton
Scilla: squill
Stachys lanata: lamb's tongue
Stipa gigantea
Thalictrum: meadow rue
Tulipa 'White triumphator'
Verbana bonariensis: vervain
Viola: violet, pansey

Climbing plants
Aristolochia
Clematis 'Madame Lecoultre'
  C. montana
  C. viticella rubra
Hydrangea petiolaris
Jasminum: jasmine
Parthenocissus: Virginia creeper
Vitis coignetiae
Wisteria

Roses
'Albéric Barbier'
'Alister Stella Gray'
'Bobbie James'
'Francis Lester'
'General Schablikine'
'Iceberg'
'Lykkefund'
'Madame Alfred Carrière'
'Penelope'
'R. Helenae'
'Rambling Rector'
'Sparrieshoop'
Rosa gallica 'Officinalis':
  Apothecary's rose

WATER GARDENS
Perennials
Alchemilla mollis: lady's mantle
Cimicifuga
Elodea
Gunnera manicata

Hemerocallis: daylily
Heracleum mantegazzianum:
  giant hogweed
Hosta
Iris kaempferi, I. laevigata,
I. pseudacorus, I. sibirica
Juncus: rush
Lunnaria annua: honesty
Lysimachia clethroides
  L. punctata: loosetrife
Lythrum salicaria: purple loosetrife
Macleaya cordata: plume poppy
Myriophyllum: water milfoil
Nymphaea: water lily
Nymphoides peltata:
  fringed water lily
Peltiphyllum peltatum:
  umbrella plant
Petasites japonicus 'Giganteus'
Polygonatum: Solomon's seal
Pontederia
Primula
Rodgersia
Sagittaria: arrowhead
Thalictrum aquilegifolium:
  greater meadow rue

Trees and shrubs
Alnus: alder
Betula jacquemonti, B. nigra: birch
Camellia
Castanea: chestnut
Fagus: beech
Hydrangea
Laburnum anagyroides
Phoenix: palm
Pieris
Populus: poplar
Quercus rubra: American red oak
Rhododendron
Salix alba: white willow
  S. alba tristis: white
  weeping willow
Sequoia

GOURMET GARDENS
Herbs and vegetables
Allium cepa: onion
Allium porrum: leek
Allium sativum: garlic
Allium schoenoprasum: chive
Anethum graveolens: dill
Angelica archangelica
Artemisia absinthium: absinthe
Artemisia dracunculus: tarragon
Beta vulgaris: beet
Brassica rapa: turnip
Chamomilla: chamomile
Cichorium endiva: endive
Cucurbita: squash
Cynara cardunculus: artichoke
Daucus carota: carrot
Foeniculum vulgare: fennel
Fragaria: strawberry plant
Lablab
Lactuca sativa: lettuce
Lamium: nettle
Levisticum: lovage
Lycopersicon: tomato
Mentha: mint
Ocymum basilicum: basil
Origanum vulgare: oregano
Petroselinum crispum: parsley
Raphanus: radish
Rheum rhaponticum: rhubarb
Rumex: sorrel
Solanum melongena: eggplant
Solanum tuberosum: potato
Spinacia oleracea: spinach
Thymus: thyme
Verbena: vervain
Zea mays: corn

Climbing plants
Clematis 'Duchess of Albany'
  C. 'Huldine'

C. 'Marie Boisselot'
C. 'Nelly Moser'
C. 'Perle d'Azur'
C. 'Prince Charles'
C. 'The President'
C. 'Vyvyan Pennel'

Flowers
Acanthus mollis
Achillea millefolium: milfoil
Aster
Centaurea cyanus: cornflower
Centranthus ruber: valerian
Cerastium tomentosum:
  snow-in-summer
Convolvulus tricolor: bindweed
Cosmos
Dahlia
Delphinium
Dianthus: pinks
Erica arboria: tree heather
Ferns
Gaura
Geranium psilostemon
Gypsophila: baby's breath
Helleborus: hellebore
Hosta
Iris
Japanese anemone
Lathyrus odoratus: sweet pea
Lobularia maritima: sweet alyssum
Papaver: poppy
Phlox
Salvia: sage
Saxifraga: saxifrage
Stachys lanata: lamb's tongue
Thymus: thyme
Tropaeolum: nasturtium
Veronica
Viola: violet, pansey

Roses
'Albéric Barbier'
'Cuisse de Nymphe'
'Félicité et Perpétue'
'Jacques Cartier'
'Roseraie de l'Haye'
'Weichenblau'
Rosa chinensis 'Mutabilis'
  Rosa moyesii 'Geranium'

Trees and shrubs
Buxus: box
Camellia
Carpinus: hornbeam
Castanea: chestnut
ficul carica: fig
Forsythia
Lavandula: lavender
Malus: apple
Prunus: cherry
Prunus armeniaca: apricot
Prunus domestica: plume
Prunus persica: peach
Pyrus: pear
Ribes: current
Rosmarinus: rosemary
Rubus: raspberry
Santolina: lavender cotton
Taxus: yew

COLLECTORS' GARDENS
Perennials and biennials
Cornus canadensis
Digitalis: foxglove
Epimedium
Erica carnea: spring heath
Ferns
Geranium macorrhizum:
  Balkan crane's bill
  G. nodosum: knotted
    crane's bill
  G. robertianum: herb Robert
  G. sylvaticum: wood
    crane's bill
Helleborus corsicus: Corsican

hellebore
H. orientalis 'Hélène'
H. orientalis 'Lucie': oriental
  hellebore
Meconopsis betonicifolia:
  Himalayan blue poppy
  M. grandis
  M. nepaulensis
  M.× sheldoni
Polygonatum: Solomon's seal
Primula 'Insriach Hybrid',
  P. helodoxa
Pulmonaria: lungwort
Sedum 'Autumn Joy': stonecrop
Tiarella

Bulbs
Allium sativum: garlic
Amaryllis belladonna
Cardiocrinum
Colchicum: meadow saffron
Crocus
Cyclamen
Fritillaria
Galanthus nivalis: snowdrop
Narcissus
Tulipa: tulip

Climbing plants
Akebia quinata
Hydrangea petiolaris
Jasminum nudiflorum: jasmine
Rosa 'Albéric Barbier'

Trees and shrubs
Acer 'Heptalobum Osakazuki': maple
Berberis 'Rosy Glow'
Betula: birch
Callistemon: bottlebrush
Camellia
Chimonanthus praecox
Cordyline australis: palm lily
Cornus: dogwood
Corylopsis pauciflora
Dimorphotheca
Dicksonia antarctica
Echium fastuosum, E. pininana
Eryngium pandanifolium
Escallonia
Eucalyptus
Gunnera manicata
Gynerium: uva grass
Hamamelis mollis: witch hazel
Hippophae
Hydrangea aspera villosa
  H. hereromalla
  H. macrophylla 'Altona'
  'Blue Deckel'
  'Burgundy Lace'
  'Heinrich Seidel'
  'Intermezzo'
  'Madame Émile Mouillère'
  'Rosea'
  'Unique'
Lonicera fragrantissima: honeysuckle
Magnolia cylindrica,
M. sprengeri diva, M. tripetala
Mahonia japonica
Malus 'Crittenden': 'Crittendon' apple
Nothofagus: southern beech
Parrotia
Phormium
Prunus
Rhododendron 'Christmas
  cheer'
  R. 'Polar Bear'
  R. 'Praecox'
  R. dauricum
  R. nobleanum
  R. racemosum
Salix sachalihensis 'Sekka':
  willow
Sambucus nigra: elderberry
Skimmia
Sorbus hupehensis
Viburnum bodnantense
V. plicatum

B I B L I O G R A P H Y

ILLUSTRATED BOOKS

CARACALLA, J.-P., *Normandy*, The Vendome Press, 1991.

DANNENBERG, Linda, *Pierre Deux's Normandy*, Crown Publishing Group, 1988.

FELL, Derek, *Impressionist Garden*, Crown Publishing Group, 1994.

JOYES, Claire, *Monet's Table*, Simon & Schuster, 1990.

JOYES, Claire, *Claude Monet: Life at Giverny*, The Vendome Press, 1985.

PLUMPTRE, George, *The Water Garden*, Thames and Hudson, 1993.

SCHINZ, Marina, and LITTLEFIELD, Suzanne, *Visions of Paradise*, Stewart, Tabori and Chang, 1985.

VALERY, M.-F., and LEVEQUE, G., *French Garden Style*, Barron's Educational Series, 1982.

GARDEN HISTORY

FISH, Margery, *We Made a Garden*, Faber & Faber, 1984

HOBHOUSE, Penelope, and TAYLOR, Patrick, *The Gardens of Europe*, Random House, 1990.

HOBHOUSE, Penelope, *Garden Style*, Little, Brown & Company, 1988.

JEKYLL, Gertrude, *The Making of a Garden*, Antique Collector's Club, 1984

LEDENTEC, Denis and Jean-Pierre, *Reading the French Garden*, MIT Press, 1990.

QUEST-RITSON, Charles, *The English Garden Abroad*, Viking (London), 1992.

MURRAY, Elizabeth, *Monet's Passion*, Pomegranate Art Books, 1989.

PAGE, Russell, *The Education of a Gardener*, HarperCollins, 1994.

THACKER, Christopher, *The History of Gardens*, University of California Press, 1979.

ZUYLEN, Gabrielle van and SCHINZ, Maria, *The Gardens of Russell Page*, Stewart, Tabori and Chang, 1992.

PLANTS AND PRACTICAL ADVICE

AUSTIN, David, *David Austin's English Roses*, Little, Brown & Company, 1993.

BATH, Trevor, and JONES, Joy, *Hardy Geraniums*, Timber Press, 1994.

BISGROVE, R., *The Gardens of Gertrude Jekyll*, Little, Brown & Company, 1993.

HOBHOUSE, Penelope, *Flower Gardens*, Little, Brown & Company, 1991.

HOBHOUSE, Penelope, *Color in Your Garden*, Little, Brown & Company, 1991.

HUXLEY, Anthony, editor-in-chief, *The New Royal Horticultural Society Dictionary of Gardening*, 4 vols., Macmillan (London), 1992.

JEKYLL, Gertrude, *Color Schemes for the Garden*, Antique Collector's Club, 1982.

KEEN, Mary, *Gardening with Color*, Random House, 1991.

MATHEW, Brian, and SWINDELLS, Philip, *The Complete Book of Bulbs*, Reader's Digest Association, 1994.

PHILLIPS, Roger, and RIX, Martin, *Shrubs*, Random House, 1989.

PHILLIPS, Roger, and RIX, Martin, *Roses*, Random House, 1989.

PROCTOR, Rob, *Perennials*, HarperCollins, 1990.

RICE, Graham, and STRANGMAN, Elizabeth, *Gardener's Guide to Growing Hellebores*, Timber Press, 1993.

STEVENS, John, *National Trust Book of Wild Flower Gardening*, Globe-Pequot Press, 1988.

VEREY, Rosemary, *Good Planting Plans*, Little, Brown & Company, 1993.

LITERATURE

BACHELARD, Gaston, *Water and Dreams*, Dallas Institutional Publications, 1983.

BARBEY D'AUREVILLY, *Oeuvres romanesques complètes*, French & European Publications, Inc., 1983.

DUMAS, Alexandre, *La Dame aux camelias*, Oxford University Press, Ltd., 1986.

FLAUBERT, Gustave, *Madame Bovary*, Penguin Classics, 1993.

HUGO, Victor, *Les Contemplations*, Schoenhof's Foreign Books, Inc., 1965.

MAUPASSANT, Guy de, *Complete Novels*, Carroll & Graff, 1992.

PRÉVERT, Jacques, *Oeuvres complètes*, French & European Publications, Inc., 1993.

PROUST, Marcel, *Remembrance of Things Past*, Random House, 1982.

GUIDES

Good Gardens Guide: *The 1000 Best Gardens in the British Isles and Europe*, Trafalgar Square, 1994.

Fodor's Brittany and Normandy, Fodor's Travel Publications, 1993.

French Rambler's Assocation, *Coastal Walks: Normandy and Brittany*, Seven Hills Book Distributors, 1990.

MCNEILL, John, *Normandy*, W.W. Norton, 1993.

Michelin Green, *Normandy*, Michelin Travel Publications, 1994.

Normandy Discover, Berlitz Publishing Co., 1994.

INDEX

Alexandre, Arsène, 22
Andlau, Hélène d', 64, 68, 69, 175
Androuet du Cerceau, Jacques, 22, 45
Aubin, M. and Mme., 62
Audiffret-Pasquier, duc d', 100
Auge, region, 14, 22, 24, 26, 29, 30, 36
Austin, David, 30, 32, 38
Azan, François, 132

Bachelard, Gaston, 134
Baechler, Franz, 22, 73
Bagneux, Adalbert de, 159
Bagneux, Anne-Marie de, 159
Bailleul, Château de, 64, 77, 81
Barbey d'Aurevilly, 14
Basses-Terres, Les, 22
Bazille, Frédéric, 8
Beaumesnil, Château de, 77
Beaumont, Élie de, 90
Beaurepaire, 18, 19
Belguise, 146
Bellevue, Jardins de, 181–182
Benech, Louis, 19, 22, 26, 29, 30, 73, 156, 158, 159
Bergé, Pierre, 73
Bessin, Le, 134
Bizy, Château de, 77, 92–94
Blanche, Jacques-Emile, 8
Bois des Moutiers, 52, 106, 108–114, 117
Bonneville, Château de, 88
Bosmelet, Château de, 105, 151
Bosmelet, Laurence de, 151
Bosmelet, Robert de, 105, 151
Boudin, Eugène, 8
Braque, Georges, 193
Bray, region, 12
Brécy, Château de, 100
Broglie, Duc de, 19
Brown, Mark, 105, 106, 117-121
Brynner, Yul, 8
Buisson, Françoise, 175, 191
Buisson, Paul 191

Caillebotte, Gustave, 42
Canon, Château de, 77, 88-92, 105
Canovas, Isabel, 22, 37, 38
Caux, region, 12, 16, 22, 36, 56, 60, 64, 84, 87, 117, 146, 151, 158, 159, 175, 181, 185
Chahine, M. and Mme Pierre., 30
Champ de La Pierre, 68, 77
Charleval, 19
Clemenceau, Georges, 140
Clément, Gilles, 38–42
Clos du Coudray, 56–60
Clos Normand, 42, 140
Comont, Denis, 145
Coquetterie, La, 159–162
Côte Fleurie, 12
Cotelle, Catherine, 60–61
Cotelle, Frédéric, 60–61
Cotentin, 12, 14, 19, 129, 132, 194, 199

Coudray, Pépinière du, 181-182
Craquelin, Samuel, 87
Cribier, Pascal, 151, 156, 159-16
Cruse, Mme., 166-168

Debussy, Claude, 8
Delbard, Henri, 30, 32
Dezallier-Argenville, Antoine Joseph, 73
Domaine de la Rivière, 22, 26–27
Duchêne, Achille, 100, 158
Durand-Ruel, 140
Duras, Marguerite, 8
Duvoux-Bouchayer, Clotilde, 50
Dyel de Vaudrocque, 84

Earl, Mrs., 108
Eve, André 52
Evrard, Doctor, 105, 185–188
Evrard, Mme., 185, 188

Ferme du Tertre, 16
Figes, Eva, 140
Fish, Margery, 105
Flaubert, Gustave, 8, 12, 151
Forrières-du-Bosc, Les 185–191

Gabriel, Château, 69, 73
Galleville, Château de, 158–159
Geslin, Isaac, 100
Gillet, M. and Mme. Robert, 158
Giverny, 22, 42–44, 124, 129, 140–145
Gramont, Elisabeth de, 8
Grange, Jacques, 73
Great Comp, 185

Haras du Pin, 77
Harcourt, duc d', 46-49
Harcourt, duchesse d', 46
Hardouin-Mansart, Jules, 77
Harnden, Peter, 124
Heudicourt, Château d', 16, 19

Jardins d'Angélique, 52–56
Jekyll, Gertrude, 105, 106, 108–114
Jellicoe, Geoffrey, 106

Knightshayes, 177

La Conté, M. and Mme. de 50
La Plesse, manoir de, 8, 29, 30
La Varende, Jean de, 8, 12, 19, 88, 94, 151
La Varende, Mme. de, 88
Lacretelle, Jacques de, 94
Lacretelle, Mme. de, 77
Lalanne, 162

Lalloz, M. and Mme. Xavier, 146
Launay, Château de, 87–88
Le Bret, Jean, 56–60
Le Nôtre, André, 77, 92, 100
Lebellegard, M. and Mme., 52
Lemonnier, Martine, 105, 175, 181–182
Lennox-Boyd, Arabella, 106
Lessay, moor, 12
Lillers, marquis and marquise de, 84
Limpiville, Château de, 84–87
Lloyd Jones, Miss, 36, 105
Lorrain, Claude, 90
Louvet, 16
Lutyens, Edwin, 105–106,108, 114

Maison Normande, 64
Mallet, Corinne, 170, 175, 192–193
Mallet, Guillaume, 19, 100, 108, 114, 192
Mallet, Mary, 19, 105, 108, 114
Mallet, Robert, 19, 192
Mallet-Bouchayer, Claire, 114
Manoir d'Ango, 117
Manoir d'Arthur, 61–62
Mansart, François, 100
Maupassant, Guy de, 8, 22, 105, 156, 170
Mézerac, family, 92
Mirbeau, Octave, 42, 44
Miromesnil, Château de, 8, 105, 152–156
Mollet, André, 100
Moltzer, Kim, 64, 81–84
Moncel, Comte de, 19
Monet, Claude, 8, 22, 42–44, 124, 140–145, 193
Mont-Saint-Michel, 170
Motte, Vincent, 170

Nacqueville, Château de, 105, 129–132
Norton, Mr. and Mrs., 105

O. Château d', 77–81
Orcher, Château d', 8, 77
Ouche, region, 12, 19, 88

Page, Russell, 22, 26, 37, 105, 106, 121, 124, 138
Patry, moor, 16
Pellerin, Éric, 194
Pellerin, Guillaume, 199
Pellerin, Marie-Noëlle, 199
Pellerin, Nicole, 194
Perche, region, 64–68, 166
Petite Rochelle, La, 64–69
Pissarro, Camille, 8
Plantbessin, 129, 134
Pontrancart, Château du, 32, 36, 105, 129, 138
Poussin, Nicolas, 90

Prévert, Jacques, 8, 199
Proust, Marcel, 8, 14, 16, 22, 129

Richert, Alain, 77, 151
Robert, Hubert, 90
Robinson, William, 129
Roper, Lanning, 105, 106
Rousseau, Jean-Jacques, 90

Saint-Laurent, Yves, 69, 73
Saint-Just, Château de, 145–146
Saint-Michel, Prieuré, 22, 30, 32
Saint-Simon, Louis de, 92
Sainte-Beuve, Colette, 134
Sassy, Château de, 73, 77, 94–100
Sellier, Jean-Claude, 175
Senneville, father, 170
Shakespeare, William, 121
Sheffield Park, 185
Sissinghurst, 185
Steiner, Rudolph, 166
Sturdza, Princesse Greta, 19, 105, 175, 177, 178, 181

Thuit Saint-Jean, Le, 191
Thury-Harcourt, 22, 46–49, 177
Tocqueville, Alexis de, 129
Tocqueville, Hippolyte de, 105, 129–132
Trébuchet, Sophie, 146
Truffaut, Georges, 42, 140

Van Trier, Harry, 192
Van Zuylen, baron, 124
Van Zuylen, baronesse Gabrielle, 124
Vandrimare, Château de, 22, 50–52
Varaville, stud farm, 105, 121, 124
Vasterival, Le, 19, 52, 105, 175, 177–178,181
Vauville, manor of, 194, 198, 199
Vauxelles, Louis, 145
Vendeuvre, Château de, 77, 81
Vendeuvre, comte and comtesse de, 81
Vexin Normand, 12, 19
Villeray, Château de, 162, 166, 170
Vogüé, comte de, 152
Vogüé, comtesse Simone de, 105, 152

Wailly, Jacques de, 170
Waravka, Patrick, 8
Whistler, James McNeill, 8
Wirth, M. et Mme. Didier, 100

Yamamoto, Doctor, 193

ACKNOWLEDGMENTS

I present my warmest thanks to those who helped me in this wonderful adventure, the proprietors of the gardens who welcomed me with generosity and gave of their time and knowledge, and to all those who helped along the way of a thousand and one encounters. I also thank sincerely the photographers and the team at Editions Flammarion for their patience and for having supported me through their competence. I don't dare list names for fear of forgetting someone.

Marie-Françoise Valéry

I would like to send my warmest thanks to M. and Mme. Charles and their daughter Daphnée who invited me to discover the art of living in the Auge; to M. Michel Bourgeois, gardener, who guided my steps toward the beautiful apple orchards; to Sister Marie-Thérèse for her invaluable help when I ascended Mont-Saint-Michel; to the proprietors of the gardens who recieved me with warmth, in particular, Mme. de Bagneux, Docteur et Mme. Evrard, Guillaume and Marie-Noëlle Pellerin, M. and Mme. de La Conté, M. and Mme. Le Bellegard.

Vincent Motte

I would particularly like to thank Ysabel and René Courcelle as well as Odile and Kim Moltzer who often recieved and advised me during my many Normandy escapades. Warm thoughts also go to Inès, my wife, and my two sons Diego and Kim. Thank you for your infinite patience All my gratitude goes equally to Brice de Roquette-Buisson who served as my assistant during certain sight-seeing trips.

Christian Sarramon

We would like to express our recognition of all the garden proprietors who so graciously opened their doors to the photographers and the author. Particular thanks to all those who made this work possible: Marc Walter, Olivier Canaveso, Margarita Mariano, Nathalie Bailleux, Diana Darley, Florence Picard, Laurence Challamel, Claire Lamotte, Marianne Rouet and Murielle Vaux.

The Publisher

PHOTO CREDITS

Photographs by Vincent Motte
cover and pages 2-3, 6-7, 8, 9, 10-11, 14 (top), 18, 19, 20-21, 22, 42, 43, 44 (top), 45, 6, 47, 48, 49, 50, 51, 52, 53, 54-55, 56, 57, 58-59, 60, 61, 62, 63, 70-71, 72, 73, 77, 87, 122-123, 124, 125, 128, 129, 130-131, 132, 133, 134, 135, 136-137, 141, 142-143, 148-149, 150, 158, 159, 160-161, 162, 163, 164-165, 171, 184, 185, 186-187, 188, 189, 190, 191, 194, 195, 196-197, 198, 199.

Photographs by Christian Sarramon
pages 1, 4, 12, 13, 14 (bottom), 15, 16, 17, 23, 24, 25, 26, 27, 28, 29, 30, 31, 32, 33, 34-35, 36, 37, 38, 39, 40-41, 44 (bottom), 64, 65, 66-67, 68, 69, 74-75, 76, 78-79, 80, 81, 82-83, 84, 85, 86, 88, 89, 90, 91, 92, 93, 94, 95, 96-97, 98-99, 100, 101, 102-103, 104, 105, 106, 107, 108, 109, 110-111, 112, 113, 114, 115, 116, 117, 118-119, 120, 121, 126-127, 138, 139, 140, 144, 145, 146, 147, 151, 152, 153, 154-155, 156, 157, 166, 167, 168, 169, 170, 172-173, 174, 175, 176, 177, 178, 179, 180, 181, 182, 183, 192, 193, 200, 201.